CARRICK IN MY TIME

AUTHOR - PADDY HARPUR

This book is dedicated to the memory of my late wife Rosemary and to our children, grandchildren and great grandchildren.

Acknowledgements

The author wishes to thank everyone who assisted in the publication of this book,
especially:

- The Arts Council Northern Ireland who assisted in the funding of this publication.
- The editorial work by my son Brendan and his colleagues in Dublin.
- To my daughter Kathleen for publishing support.
- The support and encouragement of my family.
- Dermot Cranny for his art work.
- Benedict Kiely and Dr Séamas Ó Catháin.
- To the people of Carrick and The Glen, Drumquin, Co. Tyrone.

ISBN No 1 898719 00 4

© PADDY HARPUR

Printed by Johnswood Press, Ltd. Dublin.

Published by Harpur & Crystal

PROFILE OF AUTHOR

One of five children, Paddy Harpur was born in 1913 in Unshiniagh, Drumquin in the County of Tyrone. On his father's side his ancestors came from Donegal while his mother's were Brogan and Kennedy from Mayo. The young Harpur family were devastated by the death of their mother when the youngest child was 19 months old. Times then were difficult with work hard and hours long leaving it impossible for Paddy's father to deal with it all alone. As a result Paddy, at the age of four, was 'adopted' by a kind D'arcy family. He was an independent, observant and adaptable character even then. These are the qualities which are the strength behind a man who has led a full and interesting life despite his failing sight and ultimate blindness in his sixties. He suffers from R.P. (Retinitis Pigmentosa) a hereditary eye disease which affects the retina, causing night blindness, tunnel vision and gradual loss of central vision. He knows all about adjusting to a life of darkness but he also knew the joys of reading. Now his reading is through the medium of the Talking Book Library and the benefit of tapes. The delightful trust in and devotion of a Guide Dog has ensured his mobility to meet and talk with his neighbours. His interest in people and his yearning to pass on his "life and times in his rural Tyrone" prompted him to write this book. So he records on tapes, and from his tapes this story is written.

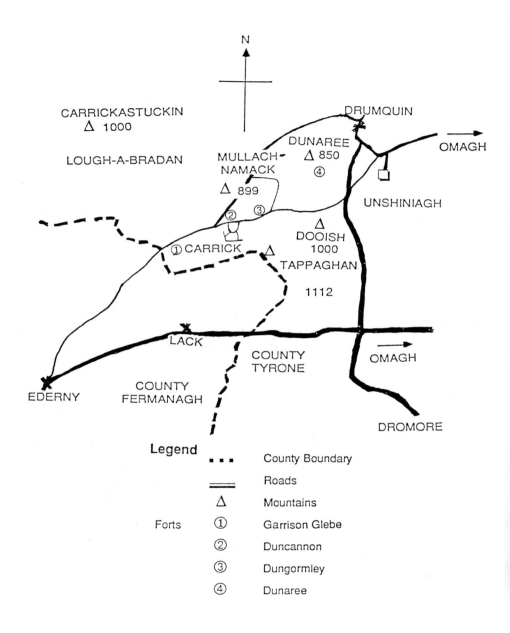

N

CARRICKASTUCKIN
△ 1000

LOUGH-A-BRADAN

DRUMQUIN

DUNAREE
MULLACH- △ 850
NAMACK ④

OMAGH

△ 899

② ③

UNSHINIAGH

① CARRICK △

△
DOOISH
1000
TAPPAGHAN

1112

LACK

COUNTY
TYRONE

OMAGH

EDERNY

COUNTY
FERMANAGH

DROMORE

Legend

· · ·   County Boundary

═══   Roads

△   Mountains

Forts   ①   Garrison Glebe

②   Duncannon

③   Dungormley

④   Dunaree

IV

FOREWORD

The vast collections amassed by the Irish Folklore Commission and its successor - the Department of Irish Folklore at University College Dublin - outstrip in quality and quantity the folklore collections of most other countries. These collections constitute an enormously important resource for the study and understanding of Irish and European culture as a whole.

Millions of manuscript pages and hundreds of hours of sound and video recordings together with thousands of photographs go to make up these collections. The material covers all manner of folk narrative (folktales, legends, proverbs, riddles etc.), folk custom and belief, memories of historical events and folk heroes of the past. The archives also contain accounts of traditional food and drink and dress, sports and pastimes - including song, music and dance - traditional tools and work practices, trade crafts and industries and much else besides. As well as describing traditional culture in all its many aspects, it may be said that the national folklore collections also provide a valuable insight into the social and economic conditions which formed the background to the everyday lives of the people in times gone by.

These collections are mainly the result of countless hours of painstaking work by a small body of full-time collectors and a network of questionnaire correspondents all over Ireland. Michael J Murphy of Dromintee in Co. Armagh was one such full-time collector who spent some time in Tyrone in the 1950s at the behest of the Irish Folklore Commission. His experiences there - particularly in the parish of Greencastle-have been described by him in *Tyrone Folk Quest* .

Through Michael J.'s efforts a good deal of the folklore of central and north-central Tyrone takes its place on the record alongside that of other parts of Ireland. Further west, however, it is a different story, as I discovered when I joined the Department of Irish folklore in 1974. To my disappointment, not a syllable or jot had ever been noted from my native parish nor had very much been done by way of collecting work in the surrounding parishes, as far as I could see.

The claim that it has all been done and that nothing remains to be collected has a particularly hollow ring to it when viewed in the context of the paucity of folklore material from west Tyrone. This is a region as richly endowed as many other parts of this island though never fortunate enough to have had its chronicler in the manner, say, in which Greencastle and district was favoured.

Since 1974, during occasional forays north, I have done my best to alter that negative profile and have had the satifaction of seeing the names of Michael McCanny of Cooel, Charlie Kearney of Dooish, Paddy McAleer, Michael O'Brien, Tom O'Kane and Tommy Quinn of Drumquin - all now deceased - as well as that of my late father, John O'Kane - joined with the names of the forty thousand or so individuals from every corner of Ireland who have made their contribution to the folklore record over the years.

With the appearance of Paddy Harpur's *Carrick In My Time*,

the parish of Longfield has now found its own unique voice. Speaking from the heart, Paddy traces the contours of what he calls 'the true landscape of Carrick'. He rightly deplores the state of his native glen as the beautiful peaks and panoramas that once so delighted his eyes succumb to the relentless uniformity imposed by large-scale schemes of afforestation.

Perhaps even more importantly, Paddy has succeeded in recreating a cultural landscape which in many respects has already disappeared from view and which, but for him, might hardly be noticed in its passing never mind stand a chance of being remembered by a new generation. With great sympathy and understanding, he articulates in his own engaging way the heroic spirit and droll and often earthy humour of the lost world in which he grew up. His account marks him and his neighbours as well as his fellow parishioners as worthy participants in the greater Irish tradition and as true representatives of it.

The role of Paddy's son, Brendan, in helping to bring his father's memoirs to the attention of a wider public must also be acknowledged with gratitude. I appreciate the opportunity which Brendan has given me to pen these few words of welcome for *Carrick In My Time* and wish it every success.

Professor Séamas Ó Catháin
Archivist
Department of Irish Folklore
University College Dublin

INTRODUCTION

For me, in my boyhood, the way to Paddy Harpur's country would be on a bike from Omagh town to Segully Crossroads. Then to the left by way of the hills above Drumquin, celebrated in song by Felix Kearney who was a friend of my mother and whom I had the honour of visiting at his home in Clanabogan on the old road from Omagh to Dromore. About which road Felix had written another song.

His name was often mentioned and his songs sung in the house of my uncle, Owen Gormley, up under the shadow of Tappaghan mountain where this fine book of memories begins. It was a great house for traditional music and the name of Harpur was among the names of the fine people who frequented it.

As a wee fellow I tramped over Tappaghan to Lough - A- Bradan, an enchanted lake or so it seemed to me, there to try to imitate my brother at casting a fly. The fish in that lovely lake were quite safe from me. But the view from up there was worth the hard walk. That view is, in these memories described in exact detail. To me it then seemed simply as if I was on the roof of the world.

Paddy Harpur describes that land, its people, their way of life and customs, most faithfully and lovingly. He makes music out of the place names or draws out what was already there. As I've said his book has a special interest for myself. But it will be of interest and value to all, scholars and ordinary people, who are interested in the ways of our rural Ireland before the changes that time brings began to speed up like crazy, as the century draws to an end. Even centuries must end. This record is priceless.

Faces and names leap out at me from these pages. Peter McCanny and his cousin, Joe. Captain Scott of Omagh and the great mill that produced Scott's Excelsior flaked oat meal. Fr. Gormley of Langfield Church, a man respected or perhaps, reverenced would be a better word. Willie Lowe who worked with my brother. Micky Doran on Cornavara who had the reputation of being a wise man and a bit of a wizard. And others. And others.

You may not have met them yet. But read on and you will be introduced. And will remember them and the places they lived in and the way they lived.

Benedict Kiely.

CONTENTS

Page No.

CHAPTER ONE

Carrick- a view from the mountain

I am a child of five years, sitting at the top of Carrick Mountain on the west slope of Tappaghan Mountain which is situated in West Tyrone. It is the first time I have climbed this mountain. There are acres and acres of corn in big fields, small fields and oddly shaped fields. These form a golden patchwork path westward through the glen and valleys and disappearing into the silver expanse of lower Lough Erne in County Fermanagh. At the end of that western horizon the steep rock cliffs which form the " Falls of Beleek" seem to stop the waters of Lough Erne from falling over the horizon. The year is 1918.

I am now eighty years old, the corn fields have gone and so has my sight. Yet in my mind I can recall that picture and every other scene on the Carrick landscape.

I can still see northwards over a mile away, down in the valley the whitewashed walls of a cluster of houses. This forms the heart of the townland of Carrick and known locally as Carrick Street.

I recall that bright clear day when the mist had been drawn back and allowed the mountain peaks to stand naked and majestic. I was eight years old and it was my first time to work at cutting turf. The turf bank was just a little way above the cross ditch on Carrick mountain.The cross ditch was a deep open drain with a three feet mound of earth along its edge. This ditch marked the boundary between individually owned strips of land and common sheep pasture.

The man on the turf spade that day was Paddy Ferry from Carrick Street who lived two doors away from me. Paddy was about sixty years of age. I had the job of lifting or filling turf from the cutter onto the wheelbarrow and shovel. A fitting job for small boys to let one know what real work would be like. I didn't mind, it was a sort of a novelty to me, a chance to be one of the men. On that warmish April day Paddy Ferry was singing his usual verse of a song,

" When gazing back at Barnes Gap
My own dear native hills
I thought no shame or who could blame
If then I cried my fill".

Paddy was being light hearted and jokingly sang his verse meaning that I had my back to Barnes Gap in Co. Donegal. I had two freshly cut turf in my hand, I stopped and straightened up, "Where is Barnes Gap anyway"? I asked Paddy. Paddy stuck the turf spade in the turf floor and

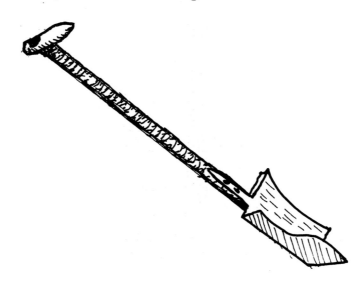

joining his hands he rested them over the top of the turf spade. He then rested his chin on his hands. Work and time stood still. Without pointing a finger Paddy explained where Barnes Gap was likely to be somewhere in those distant range of mountains in the Northwest. That day and following days Paddy Ferry explained the geography of the surrounding countryside. He interpreted for me the historic significance of clumps of bushes on little hills and how streams and ditches marked the boundaries of townlands. He talked about old times and of people long dead and gave me an appreciation of the people and the community of Carrick and the Glen. Later I will tell you something about the people and the folklore of this area. For now in my minds eye I will take you for a ramble in this historic and beautiful Glen in Tyrone.

CHAPTER TWO

A Ramble in the Glen

From my imaginary seat on top of Carrick Mountain I can see a transparent cloud of bluish turf smoke hanging over the brown thatched roofs. One, two, three and that's my house sending up its little independent stream of smoke. On the far side of the Glen the large hill of Mullinamac peers down at Carrick Street. A little to the right is Carrickard, a small peak at the top of what is known locally as Donnelly's Croft. Further north at a slightly higher altitude is the townland of Proughlish. The brown and purple land now rises to the brown peak of Carrickastoken. A little to the left in the foreground about five miles away the saucer shaped Lough Bradan, locally called Lough-a-Bradan. In the distance beyond Lough-a-Bradan a deep bluish triangle appears. That's the top of Errigal mountain over sixty miles away in County Donegal. The locals call it the "Cock of the North". Moving anti-clockwise I follow the rim of the horizon in the north west. I see what looks like a lap of hay with a wee lap on top. That's Muckish Mountain. A little further to the left is Blue Stack Mountain befitting its name as it looks like a miniature turf stack as a backdrop to the intervening hills.

The western sun sprays out from behind the Falls of Beleek plunging shafts of light into Lough Erne and it's difficult to distinguish which are shafts of light and which are the cliff faces. I can see in this western view the village of Ederny in County Fermanagh, about five miles away. I survey my neighbouring townlands of Curragh, Meenaheeri, Marrock, Tirmacspird, Gortnasole, Annalough, Garrison Glebe and the adjoining townland of Carradowa.

To get a better view of the lumpy shaped Culciagh Mountains I walk southwards over the crest of the mountain. From here the land sweeps down, spreads wide and rises to the source of the River Shannon in Country Leitrim. At this viewing spot a long open ditch runs east to west. This is the county boundary between Tyrone and Fermanagh. It's a great thrill to be able to jump over the ditch from one county to another!

The southwest butt of Tappaghan Mountain prevents me from seeing any further south or southeast. As I climb northeastwards I can see the tip of the spire on the Sacred Heart Church in the county town of Omagh. That is about twelve miles away. I now have a full view of this historic glen running eastwards from Carrick to my nearest village, Drumquin in County Tyrone. The corn fields are like yellow ribbons on either side of the glen road. The rising fields reflect the quality of the soil and stages of ripening as the yellow corn fades into deepening shades of green. Then the colours abruptly change to brown heather clad hills on the adjoining townland of Carrickbwee. The ancient ring fort of Dunaree juts out at the end of a range of hills from Clunahill overlooking the townland of Cooel. Beneath the fort is Cooel Wood where hazelnuts will be plentiful for Halloween. Dunaree was once used as one of a chain of signal forts used by the O'Neills, Earls of Tyrone .

The chain of forts ran from the borders of Maguires' Fermanagh to O'Neill's headquarters in Dungannon. Moving westwards I can see the links up the Glen, Dunaree, Dungormley on the eastern end and Duncannon on the western end of Carrick and right up to the Fermanagh border there is the fort at Garrison Glebe. It's now I can identify these historic spots which fascinated me when talked of by my foster parents and the various storytellers in the locality.

One of the earliest stories I heard was of a battle between the forces of O'Neill of Tyrone against Maguire at Lough Erne. Maguire was supported by the O'Donnells of Donegal and O'Neill was forced to make a retreat down through the Glen and through the townland of Carrick. This battle is reputedly recorded in the Annals of the Four Masters. At that time there were only two houses in the Glen, one in the townland of Tirmacspird just inside County Fermanagh and the other three miles away at Ann's Brae on the eastside of the Glen.

There is a local piece of folklore connected with this retreat. O'Neill in desperation was supposed to have buried three goat skins of gold somewhere north of Carrick on the opposite northern hillside. The location can be found by discovering a certain marker stone on the hillside east of Carrick Street and following a path northwards. However, gold diggers should beware. O'Neill is supposed to have got a man to swear that he was to guard the gold living or dead. After the guard took the oath he was killed and buried with the gold.

As I look at the old fort of Dunaree I am reminded of one of the stories told to me by a local man named Mick Connolly. Mick Connolly Senior told me something of the history of the old church at Liskey near Drumquin. At one time Catholics attended Mass in the morning and their fellow persecuted brothers the Presbyterians, worshipped in the Church in the afternoon. This was the period of the Napoleonic Wars when conscription was being enforced. The United Irishmen who were active at that time were camped about three miles away in Cooel Wood near the old fort of Dunaree from which they had a good vantage point.

When police came to collect Presbyterians they fled to Cooel Wood to join the United Irishmen. The police had to leave without their recruits and the army was dispatched from Belfast.

The troops occupied Liskey Church. The combined forces of the United Irishmen and the Presbyterians attacked and dispersed the military. The church was burned in this battle and left derelict since. It was then that the Catholics moved to the present site of the old St. Patrick's Church in the townland of Langfield. At that time Mass was celebrated in a barn in a garden owned by a man named McNabb, later owned by Healys. A new church was erected in 1835 under the direction of a priest named Father Starrs. The architect for the church was a Dublin man and he was paid £50 for his efforts. It would appear that he underpriced the job because he is supposed to have died in the poor house a short time later.

It is with sadness that I have to record that the old St. Patrick's Church, we called it the Chapel, was demolished in 1992. Not a trace of its walls remain. The following verses is my lament for the disappearance of the old Chapel.

In Memory of St. Patrick's Old Church - Langfield

The old church at Langfield has vanished
In sorrow we all saw it go,
Once it stood like a gem in the valley
Our forefathers loved beauty so
From the strong hand of time it had weakened,
Those walls which were once strong and high
When its windows in sunshine did sparkle
It was cherished by all who passed by

We watched as the lorries assembled,
Great Diggers and Cranes they were there
Their powerful engines were roaring
The old church was no longer there
Our thoughts went back to the builders
When the big wheels they trundled along
Their labours shone out from those dark years
They are honoured in story and song

When the old church was finished it stood there,
All aflame in the morning sunshine
When the people walked forth on a Sunday
Raised their hats when they heard the bells chime
For each had a hand in the building
For the parish had gathered around
Cut stone on the front it stood there
By a law then a mile from the town

Many dead some are living that prayed there
Some are scattered far over the seas
They'll be sad when the message it finds them

That the old church will no longer be
Many weddings and funerals were held there
Our exiles will now shed a tear
For the memory of losing their loved ones
Who are laid in the churchyard so near

The old church has seen many changes
Since erected by one Father Starrs
Fifteen years before the great famine
Who got builders from Dublin so far
Many children have been baptised there
First Communioon and their first prayers
And later they had Confirmation
For them to fulfil the Lord's Prayer

The North wind it sweeps down the valley
Around the churchyard now looking so bare
And no one will know that it stood there
And in time there'll be no one to care
But you cannot demolish a memory
Or feelings that run deep in the heart
St. Patrick's Old Church there in Langfield
Is a vision that n'er will depart.

The construction of this church has a connection with Carrick in that the trees on the site were cleared by a Carrick man called Haughey. He was building a new two-storey house. Haughey decided to transport the newly felled timber with a young mare and cart. The britchin used on the horses at that time were made of rushes. Haughey had to transport the load of timber on what is now the old road from Drumquin to Carrick, up Glenbann over Clunahill and over the high rise of Mullinamac.

It was when he was coming down one of the steep hills close to Connolly's Lane and in sight of his new home that tragedy struck. The rush britchin broke, the load slipped forward. In the panic, Haughey went in front of the mare to hold her but one of the heavy timbers slid forward and killed him instantly. The mare bolted and ran some distance dispensing of the cart and returned to stand over her slain master. The Haughey homestead now stands as a single storey dwelling, as the house plan was changed as a result of his death.Haughey became the first person to be buried in the graveyard which was then the site of the new Langfield Church. His grave is located near the north-eastern corner of the graveyard surrounding the church.

I now focus on the fields of my own farm. The fields all have their own names. There is the Loop, the Underloop, the Upperloop, the Bottom, the Curragh, the Meadow and Garryveen which is a strip of ground on the west side of the big hay meadow.

Some of my neighbours' fields also have their own identities. To the right at the foot of the mountain on Ferry's land is a field called 'Patahourican'. Behind Carrick Street, a big field called the Pairc and East of Carrick on Tom 'Mor' Mc Canny's land is a field called ' The Brannan'. Behind the

'Brannan' just inside the townland of Carrickbwee on John 'Charley's' McElholm's ground is a garden with a large rock called 'Garryowen'.

I laugh to myself when I think of a field called Dan's Oldhole beside the stream in Carrick. Dan Ferry's neighbour, Catherine Darcy had a field called 'the bottom'. As a child it was great fun to talk about Dan's Old Hole and Kate's Bottom!.

It is now time to leave my imaginary seat and journey downwards. The squelching green moss and the scratching of heather bristles against my wellingtons are exaggerated sounds in the stillness of the countryside. As I descend this mountain my view gets restricted. It is like sliding down the inside of a big bowl. Lough-a-Bradan changes from being the glazed oval Lough to a short horizontal strip of grey and it is gradually disappearing with each step I take.

Lough-a-Bradan in the townland of Ally reminds me that there is an ancient passage grave and Cairn located there. It also reminds me that one of the Ceiliers to my house once lived near there. In spirit I pass the Fairy Bush, an old blackthorn standing lonely on the march ditch which divides our land from our neighbours. My thoughts turn to the people close to me, my foster parents, the Ceiliers, the storytellers and the Carrick community.

CHAPTER THREE

A youngster in Carrick

I was born in the townland of Unshiniagh in a small cottage consisting of two rooms in a wee area we called Crockalabin. My earliest memory is of my mother when I was three years of age. Another woman was visiting her and I got upset about something and I was crying. I remember my mother picking me up and sitting me on her knee and comforting me with a cuddle. My mother died when I was four years old.

My eldest brother Johnny, was then ten years old. I also had an elder sister, Maggie another sister Mary and the youngest was Willie, he was aged eighteen months. Johnny although only being ten years old had already served two years as a hired hand to a local farmer. For a while my father tried to keep our young family together. He worked all day for two shillings, he used to come home and bake bread and get the supper. He would then get the younger ones to bed and went out again and flailed corn in barns until midnight to earn extra money. His eyesight was failing and he realised that in our best interests the family would have to be split up. The youngest of eighteen months went to my mother's brother, Willie Brogan and his family. My eldest brother stayed with the farmer to whom he was hired . The farmer's name was Turner and he had a niece who also lived there. She was a little older than my brother. Turner had an arrangement where he alternated work and school on a daily basis with his niece and my brother.

Unfortunately, we had not many relatives living nearby. My father's family was from Donegal and my mother's family had come from Mayo at the time of the Famine. I was fostered, though I prefer to use the term adopted, by an elderly couple called Catherine and Barney Darcy, who lived in Carrick Street.

I remember being dressed up and taken by them in one of the only two motor cars in Drumquin at that time. Mick Donnelly was a car driver and owner, a reddish-haired man with a moustache. I was surprised when he arrived with, as I then thought, an old couple to collect me. I remember other children coming in to see the new arrival in my new home. One of the first things my new parents asked me on arrival was to sing. My father was well known in the Drumquin area as a good singer. I remember singing the "Star of Donegal". They were very pleased. From then on, this was my party piece for my proud new parents. Catherine Darcy was a tidy strict housekeeper. She was about five foot five inches in height, a sturdy good-looking woman who held her head high. She always appeared ready to go and tackle any situation. She was also a very industrious person. Barney Darcy was a stout strong-looking man. Although he looked big to me he may not have been more than of average height. He was very determined and fierce looking but he was very fond of children. I became very attached to him. Children were very fond of Barney and regarded him as one of themselves. However, if a man annoyed him he was capable of being a fearsome person. Whenever children were around, Barney took on a different personality. He would jump and play, run races and take them fishing. Barney was not a man for long conversations. He was quiet and patient and never said a cross word to me even though I used to pester him with questions or wanting to help him with his work.

I remember one day I followed him to work in the fields. I was about five years old. Barney wanted me to go home as it was a very cold day. Like all small boys I wanted to be working like an adult and I refused to go home. Barney brought me over to the high ditch which sheltered the field.He cut a long flat stick and showed me how to poke a wee opening in the hedge and for me to create an imaginary wee house I could play in.

Barney once made me a slide car. He cut a small sapling off a tree which had it's trunk forked out into two branches. The branches acted as handles which I stood between. Barney nailed a flat board onto the trunk behind and drove a steel pin in the trunk so that it would act as a tie point on which to tie my small loads and prevent them slipping off. I used to take my slide car when Barney was cutting turf. Barney would place one turf on it for me. I would then draw it out and unload the turf on the turf bank.

I remember one day Barney took me up to the field at the foot of the mountain called the Loop to inspect a few calves grazing there. At the entrance to this field there is a small flat grassy spot. To the right a deep shough (drain) which drained the water off Carrick Mountain and was always in constant flow. It was a beautiful sunny day. Barney took out his penknife and stuck it in the middle of this flat green spot. Then he started to toss coins towards what he called "The Bab". Pitch and Toss was a popular pastime in the area and Barney was having a practice session.

Barney was also fond of fishing. However he didn't use rod nor line. He preferred to wade in the stream and reach under stones and catch the fish with his hands which he called 'Ginnelin Trout'. Another day Barney took me up Carrick Mountain to clamp turf. The curlews were calling

27

which was a sign of rain. A rush was on to finish building a clamp before the rain came. Barney had shown me how to carry armfuls of turf to the clamp. However I felt in this emergency it was better to throw the turf from a distance and land them around Barney's feet. He wasn't pleased. Fortunately for me a sudden cloudburst sent us running home and my misdemeanour was forgotten.

There were small things which Barney did which I appreciated. Children were never given an egg for breakfast but Barney would cut his egg in half and give it to me. Barney showed me how to make rod baskets and creels. I remember making my first creel. Based on my observations of Barney's methods I stuck twenty four rods in the ground in a rectangular formation. I attempted the mouth knot which is an anchor point in weaving the finer rods around the upright sticks. I eventually completed a rather makeshift creel and I called Barney to pull the creel out of the ground. The twenty four stake rods were well inserted into the ground. Barney's big hands and arms reached around the creel and with great patience and care he managed a mini miracle to unearth the creel intact. He made no comment about the condition of the creel but his actions said it all. My first attempt was worthy of being handled as though it were a masterpiece.

Barney went out one Spring to prepare the ground for potatoes. On one of the lazy beds or ridges he discovered a rabbit that had a nest of young. Barney did not disturb the mother and her young but worked around the nest. This was typical of Barney's tenderness.

Barney died of heart failure. I remember his painful laments coming from the bedroom and the shock of seeing him spit blood. Barney must not have been well before I came. I concluded I was part of a long term plan to be company for Catherine after his death. Barney Darcy died in January, 1923. I remember the horse-drawn hearse coming up the lane. The driver wore a top hat and the horses looked frisky and lively. It was a dry frosty morning. I remember having been sent the previous day to tell William McLoughlin of Cornashesk about Barney's death. I was given directions of how to get there and how to cross over rivers and over a single stick which was a crude bridge or usually called a foot stick. I remember the shock and sadness on William's face when I told him about Barney. For me I could not believe Barney had died. I was left at home for the funeral. I missed him a lot.

Barney's wife Catherine had a hard up-bringing and felt that the next generation should sample the same. She was strong, believed in strong discipline and that children should immediately obey commands. This approach never seemed to have a positive influence on me. Although she was very firm and stern she never hit me. Catherine was a very generous person when it came to food. A factor that may have influenced her was the fact that her parents survived the Great Famine. She told me that the local people went to a glen behind Tappaghan Mountain and gathered sorrel which was all they had to eat when the potatoes failed.

I remember when I first came to live with her, she used to give me a cup of tay(tea), and a wee small piece of bread before I got out of bed in the morning. Then I would get up to my breakfast which consisted of a slice of a three inch thick baked scone and more tay. I didn't like this bread. I preferred the pan baked bread which was baked in a flat frying pan. This had a nice hard tasty crust. Dinner consisted of a solid two and a half inch square by a half inch thick chunk of bacon. I might also have watery vegetable soup and spuds (potatoes). As Friday was a day of abstinence there was no bacon. Instead when I came home from school the spuds would be sitting being roasted in front of the hearth with their floury hearts bursting out.

After Barney died I remember Catherine taking me up to the mountain for a bag of turf. She filled a hession sack full of turf and then wrapped a clod in the mouth of the bag which acted as a knob to hold onto when the sack was upon her back. I was allowed to carry four turf in my sack. As she handed me the sack she advised me that "small loads make good drawing horses".

Even though Barney was gone there were other local men who took an interest in me. One man was a neighbour of ours called Dan Ferry. Dan taught me how to snare rabbits and hares. He told me that at the time of the Famine people used to snare birds using a horse's hair.

Blackbirds were the most common to snare as they were plentiful. They were attracted by grubs in the thatch. Blackbirds were regarded as legitimate targets as their excavation of grubs in the thatch caused many a leaking thatched roof. In the wintertime it was regular to see a small pyramid shaped basket called a claven. The base was about twelve inches square and its height was nine inches. This was used as a trap to catch blackbirds. This little pyramid was delicately propped up by a fork twig just high enough for a blackbird to walk in. This was connected on the inside to a semi-circular springlike sally rod. The blackbird would be attracted by crumbs and it had only to touch the spring and down came the pyramid. Robins, finches and other small birds were released but blackbirds were eaten.

Dan Ferry called the snares for rabbits and hares a "Dull".

The dull was made from pleating together two strands of fine copper wire. A noose was then made and this was tied to a small stake or balkin by a piece of twine. A rabbit's path was distinguishable from a hare's in that it had bumps and hollows caused by the rabbit bouncing along, whereas the hare had a continuous worn path. For a rabbit the loop of the dull was set the width of a hand high above the ground in the rabbit's landing spot. For a hare the loop was set higher about the full length of one's hand from the wrist to the point of the middle finger. One had to ensure that the restraining string and balkin were concealed in the undergrowth.

I got a little pup. She was blue, black and with a white ring around her neck. She had a white stripe down her face. I called her Beauty. Beauty used to get caught in my rabbit snares. She used to lie there quietly until I came and released her.

One day Catherine was carrying a bag of turf down the mountain and she caught her foot in one of my snares. She toppled over sending the bag of turf rolling down the

31

mountain side.

I remember feeling frightened in case she had hurt herself as it would have been my fault for setting a snare on a human's path.

Some years after Barney's death Catherine befriended a man from Bundoran. She was at the point of remarrying but declined as the prospective husband never gave any consideration for me. I suppose she must have loved me quite a lot.

Times were hard and people were poor. Most farmers had about 25 acres with half of it in mountain pastures. Barney in earlier years went to work in England during the Summer in order to have enough money to survive. Barney and Catherine were a happy couple and one little memory sums up their closeness. Catherine had become addicted to tobacco when she had to nurse an old aunt who smoked a pipe. Catherine used to have to light the pipe for her. The aunt became bedridden and was afraid of lighting the pipe in case she put the bed on fire. Consequently Catherine became addicted to the clay pipe.

Whenever there was a visitor in the house, Barney and Catherine would disappear into the bedroom for about ten minutes. This I knew was for Catherine to share a few puffs on Barney's pipe. The neighbours knew what was going on and would smile whenever the pair would head for the bedroom.

When I was still a youngster in Carrick there was a local young man named Paddy Muldoon. I used to love to see Paddy coming to my house. Paddy was the local barber. On Saturday evenings he would provide this free social service for seven or eight customers. Paddy used to pay me two pence if I went a two mile journey to buy tobacco for him. A generous payment considering that at that time a day's pay for a labouring man was two shillings.

Then there was the day Paddy Muldoon started to tease me. I decided a well aimed stone would sort him out. It hit him on the shin just below the knee. Paddy grasped his injured knee with both hands and danced around on the other leg. A painful blow. I kept my distance until the injured leg touched the ground. Then I ran as fast as I could. Paddy did not catch me and for a few weeks we kept our distance and then it was all forgotten.

As a youngster I had always my share of chores around the farm. I remember on summer mornings rising at six o'clock and going down to the meadow to milk two or three cows. Then I had to take the cows and herd them about a half a mile to the foot of the mountain. This I did before breakfast and then went on to school. In the Autumn, when I returned from school I was sent out to pick the poreens, the small potatoes left in the ridges after Catherine had gathered the large potatoes earlier in the day. Another evening job was to put in the ducks and hens for the night.

This reminds me of a neighbouring young woman who also had the job of putting in the ducks. One wet evening she had a secret rendezvous with my friend Paddy Muldoon. She got a small creel and trapped the duck in the corner of the field well away from her home. She came running back shouting "Mammy, Mammy the grey duck is missing". Her mother gave her an overcoat to go and search for the lost duck. Two hours later on her way back from courting she picked up the duck from under the creel and returned home with the grey duck under her arm. Her mother sang the praises of how her daughter had searched rivers and fields to retrieve the grey duck.

I remember getting my first spade at nine years of age from William McVeigh. William took an old spade trimmed it with a cold chisel and a heavy hammer. I turned the handle on the grind stone as he ground the sharp edge on the spade. He shortened the handle of the spade to suit my height. For a nine year old to have to dig and set spuds may have appeared harsh but for me at that time it was an enjoyable task.

SCHOOL

My school was Loughmulhern School and it was built in 1878. It was a stone building with large chimneys at each end. Its capacity was to seat about 80 children. It consisted of one large room, wooden floor and a surround of tongue and grooved panelling around the walls. It had two fire grates, one at each end which in my time burned turf. Turf supplies were transported daily by the school children. An extension porch was added in 1933. The school has since been converted to a modern dwelling house. The local legend regarding the origin of the name Loughmulhern was that a couple named Mullan and Herren eloped and in the process of evading capture were drowned in a lough near to where the school is situated. The lough was on Gorman's land now owned by Gallogally in the townland of Garrison Glebe. The lough has since been drained.

The school before the Loughmulhern school was located about 500 yards away across the fields in a place known locally as "Divin's Land". The name came from a family named Divin who were evicted from Baronscourt near Newtownstewart, County Tyrone. The record of this eviction is noted in "The Abercorn Letters". This school in turn succeeded the first government recognised school which was situated near Corlishog Bridge. Schools before that time were held in private houses. One was in the home of Tom Connolly who lived in Carrick Street and another one in a house owned by a family called Sheridan. I don't know what the official status of these schools were but it was known that they had visits from school inspectors.

I remember my first day at school. It was a bright sunny morning and I can still hear the birds singing in the trees on the roadside near Holland's Rock. A big carefree girl called Sadie Ferry held me by the hand on the way to school. My first impression of my teacher was that she had a broadish big nose with a sharp point. Her nose was like a large hen's beak and reminded me of a hen that was about to peck someone. She wore a red knitted pullover which I later discovered was a great target for burrs (small prickly balls which came off a shrub locally called a burr bush) to stick on when thrown at her back when she was writing on the blackboard. The image I had prior to attending school, which unfortunately was borne out to some extent, was one of going to a prison or torture house. The building was cold and grey inside and out. Well, if the building was cold and grey it symbolised the coldness of the teacher's personality. Apart from the physical punishment meted out her bouts of ridiculing your family hurt even more. School became a lesson in survival. I was quickly to learn that the punishment for forgetting to bring the daily requirement of two turf was to sit and shiver with other poor souls opposite the big hole in the front door.

Going to school I got a 'Slouder'. This was a slice off a three inch scone of dry bread and I dropped it into to my schoolbag unwrapped. No fancy wrappings or tinfoil then. During class at school I kept the slice of scone in my jacket pocket and nibbled away. This was to ensure that I had the maximum time available at lunch time for playing and not using up important playtime by eating.

The teacher had her son in my class. He was very popular due to his loyalty to his classmates. He would never tell tales to his mother. We always seemed to be cold in school. Most children had a runny nose. Sleeves were used as handkerchiefs when several snorts up the nostrils failed to contain the flow. Then there was a Mr. Robb who was a school attendance inspector. No one liked to see him coming.

There was a schools inspector feared by the teacher and then there was the ecclesiastical inspector. The ecclesiastical inspection was once a year and was conducted by a priest from the diocese of Derry. I remember one lad at school who was preparing for the annual ecclesiastical inspection. He was studying at home a passage from scripture where Christ had said to Peter " Upon this rock I shall build my church and the gates of Hell shall not prevail against it. Feed my lambs, feed my sheep". The lad's father would jokingly intervene and add "and throw a lock of hay to the donkey". As fate would have it the ecclesiastical inspector asked this boy to quote this scriptural passage. The boy obliged and without hesitation completed the passage with the line "and throw a lock of hay to the donkey".

It was the custom for us children to go barefooted to school from the first day of May. Our parents discouraged this practice. However we would leave home wearing shoes and then hide our shoes in the hedge and collect them on the way home again. The thrill in our barefeet was that we could run faster and wallow in muddy patches and watch the mud squelch up between our toes. Of course we would

36

end up with our legs all mud and this would dry and cake in the dry weather. This would necessitate a visit to the nearest stream where fine sand was used as a detergent to remove the stubborn caked earth.

I remember coming from school and the road had been edged. That meant the sods which had grown onto the edge of the road would have been lifted and turned over by a Council worker. These edgings provided great ammunition for sod fights. Sod fights were also commonplace at lunchtime in the school yard. On one occasion in class I raised my hand to be excused to go to the toilet. The teacher shouted at me to "put down that sod, Pat Harpur". That is how dirty my hands had become from a lunchtime battle.

It was not unusual for a dog to follow it's young master or mistress to school. Dogs would excitedly meet their young handlers at the end of lanes or some other regular greeting place between home and school. One day there was a knock at our school door. Our lady teacher glanced in the mirror, tidied her hair and opened the door. In trotted a black and white sheepdog who went and lay down by the side of his delighted schoolboy owner.

The quality of the English language spoken at home compared to that in school was interesting. Partly this was a resistance to being Anglified. Yes and no became aye and naw, door became dure, floor became flure, stack and stek, tea was tay (té). These were some examples of the differences which still exist to the present day.

I remember at one time the school was closed for three months because a fever had swept the area. It was a welcome relief for us all. I was thirteen and a half years when I left school.

CHAPTER FOUR

The community

At that time people never locked their doors. In fact people would be offended if you knocked on the door before entering. Knocks on doors were for policemen. If people were leaving the house empty they would simply put a piece of rod through the handle beside the door latch, just to let the neighbours know that everyone was gone. I remember this old couple who used to go to bed in the middle of the day. If one went into the house the old woman would emerge from the bedroom and apologise for keeping you waiting. She then would make the excuse that she had been just outside looking for hen's nests.

A characteristic of good neighbourliness was to loan their "clocker". The "clocker" or set hen did the business of hatching chickens before the coming of incubators.

There was also a system of community welfare in operation. Groups of men would gather up and cut turf and win the hay for a widow woman. The sick always had visitors. If a woman was sick all the women in the townland and further afield would go and visit her. If a baby was being born there was a great fuss altogether and the women would be tripping over each other and lifting the baby and commenting on its looks.

People were in constant contact as there were always people out working in fields or going to the wells for water. They would shout conversations from field to field.

Some houses even had a connecting door with their neighbours. There were various explanations for this door. Some thought they were designed for a quick escape for a man on the run. Others believed that they were a convenience for nocturnal exchanges of partners in true community spirit!.

There was an unwritten code of practice concerning children. If a child came to a house and its clothes were torn the woman of the house would mend the child's clothes. This was because the child's mother might be ill and this was an act of goodwill. A child visiting a house on an errand never left without a 'capper'. This was a slice of homemade bread with homemade butter and sometimes even jam. These were some of the norms of the Carrick community.

Scarlet Fever swept through Carrick around 1917. There was one sad case where a man and his two sons died at the same time leaving a widow and a daughter. In 1918 there was a Flu Epidemic over Europe and Carrick did not escape. All the families were in bed and the old people were raving with the fever. Doctors were rarely called. If you heard that a priest and doctor were called to someone you knew that they were going to die. A doctor's call then cost a pound.

Babies were delivered by a local "handywoman" who acted as midwife. There was the occasion once where a group of men and women were shearing corn in a field near Corlishog Bridge. One of the women was pregnant and the baby was due. The group knew this and were keeping a watchful eye on her as the work was tough. Next thing happened was that the woman went missing. After a short search they found her behind a stook of corn nursing her new born infant. Interesting to note that burnt straw and later white flour were used as baby powder.

The role of the local "handywoman" or midwife took on a greater significance for one young lad. He wasn't too bright and had often heard discussed at home that a Mrs.

Weir had delivered him as a baby when he was born. Now Mrs. Weir was known only as "Long John's woman" to distinguish her from all the other Mrs Weirs. The young lad who was not very well versed in his Catechism was asked by the ecclesiastic inspector "who created you and placed you in this world?". Quick as a flash the young lad replied, " Long John's woman".

There was a tragic story of a young woman who had a two year old daughter and she was expecting her second child. One night she baked a scone of bread and put it on a plate on the table to cool. She took ill and the husband set out on foot for a doctor. The woman went to bed but decided to get up again but she went into labour and collapsed on the floor and gave birth to her second daughter. Unfortunately there were only a couple of doting old women in the house at the time and they panicked. They got a neighbouring man to lift the woman back into her bed which tragically contributed to her instant death. In the space of fifteen minutes the new baby arrived, the young woman had died, and the scone of bread was still steaming on the table.

Most families had a donkey. Apart from being a beast of burden and of very practical use around a farmhouse the donkey was the children's favourite pet. One family had a donkey who used to play "dead" with the children. When the donkey would see the children coming for rides he would lie down, close his eyes and pretend he was dead. All the proddings and encouragement of the children would not work. The children had their plan, they would come with some bread and leave it beside the donkey. The children would go off and hide at a spot where they could view the donkey. The donkey thinking that the coast was clear would raise his head and look around and then get up

41

and eat the bread.

The children would then break cover and rush cheering to their old pet and enjoy their little rides on his back.

Dogs were also a part of the family. Every house in the townland had at least one dog. A neighbour of mine Mick Connolly had a dog whom he trained to carry a milk can of tea from the house to the fields where he was working. The dog acted as a messenger between him and the house. If he needed something from the house he would write a note and tie it to the dog's collar and the dog would return with the item, be it his matches, pipe or tobacco that he had left behind.

This dog also used to enjoy rides on the mare's back as she would gallop around the paddock. He wasn't as keen about the donkey as it went too slow. He would jump off, give the donkey a nip and the donkey would gallop and then the dog would jump back up on the donkey's back. Connolly's dog was also very sensitive. If he was scolded he would huff and not be seen for two or three days.

There was a man called McCanny who had two very clever dogs. He used to drive cattle to Omagh Railway Station with the dogs. This was the first stage of a journey to a farm outside Glasgow in Scotland. He would take one dog with him on the journey via the cattle boat from Derry. After a number of trips the Scottish farmer who took delivery of the cattle was impressed with McCanny's dog. He asked McCanny if he could keep the dog for a week. McCanny agreed and showed him the signal to give to the dog when the week was up.

At the end of the week the Scotsman duly gave the dog the signal for home. Off went the dog and got on the boat at Glasgow, arrived in Derry, took the train for Omagh. Instead of travelling all the way to Omagh he got off at Newtownstewart and made his way home through the fields to Drumquin and then up to Carrick Glen. On another occasion McCanny had a group of cattle ready for Drumquin Fair. However on the morning of the fair McCanny overslept and awoke to find the dogs and cattle gone. He yoked his horse and trap and overtook the dogs and cattle near Drumquin.

FAMILIES

Before the Great Famine of 1842 there were eighteen dwellings in Carrick Street with a population of a hundred and four. The most common family names in Carrick at that time were, Connolly, Darcy, Haughey, Ferry and Maguire. Further back the names McCabe, Couple and O'Kane were popular. I knew five generations of the Connolly family.

There was a woman called Hannah Mimniagh who had a family of six children. Her husband had emigrated to Australia and died after a few years. Later Hannah and her entire family went to Australia. The story of her emigration was sorely lamented by the locals to the extent that it was still talked of thirty years later.

There were two families in Carrick which Paddy Ferry told me about. He could not remember their names but in one family there were twelve boys and one girl and twelve girls and one boy in the other family. Six of the boys and six of the girls from these two families emigrated to America on the same day.

I have written the following verses which I feel capture the thoughts of those emigrants as they left Carrick and made their way through the village of Drumquin on their way to the emigrant ships in Derry.

Leaving Drumquin

I'm leaving old Ireland tomorrow
To cross o'er the dark rolling sea
Far away from the hills and the mountains
Where the heather grows purple and free

As I pass down the road through the village
In the beautiful County Tyrone
Drumquin I will never forget you
It's the place I will always call home

Goodbye to the high hills of Kirlish
With it's copper rocks still undefiled
And the church to the west of the village
Where long ago I prayed as a child

The heather clad summit of Dooish
Where oft on a bright summer's day
I gazed o'er the hills and the valleys
To Mount Errigal so far far away

I'll remember that trim little cottage
Where it stood by the side of the stream
And the soft primrose path through the tall trees
To me such a wonderful dream

But my ship it is steadily moving
As she heads for the wild ocean foam
Where thousands have gone there before me
Saying Goodbye to old Ireland and home

If ever I come back to Ireland
To the hills of the hazel and whin
I'll build me a neat little cottage
On a hill overlooking Drumquin

There I'll hear the sweet song of the linnet
And the lark as it soars high above
And never again I'll go roaming
From the dark high hills that I love.

NICKNAMES

The name McCanny was very common in the area and therefore nicknames were attached to distinguish the various families. These were known as the "Grooms", "the Neillys", "the Red Franks", "the Neds", "the Shops", "the Jacks" and the Oineys. Oineys was taken from the Irish name ÓhEoghain. Most nicknames were attached to the family's grandfather or great great grandfather.

The name "Groom" originated when on one occasion a member of that family of McCanny was getting married. A group of men were working in a field near the Glen Road. They were watching for the McCanny man who was on his way to the church to get married. When McCanny appeared, one of the men shouted "there's the groom, there's the groom". From that day onwards the nickname "Groom" was attached to that family.

Another common name in the Carrick area were the McElholms, pronounced locally as Mac El-Holl-Um which was closer to the pronunciation of the Irish version of the name Mac Giolla Choilm. Nicknames for these families were the "Charlies" as a lot of their forefathers were called

Charles McElholm. There were the "Long Charlies", the "Yellow Charlies", the "Black Charlies" and I married a daughter of "John Charlie".

MATCHMAKING AND MARRIAGES

When I came to Carrick in 1918 matchmaking was coming to an end. Runaways (elopements) were also fading away. When a man was looking for a wife he set off with a matchmaker usually with a pint of whiskey. The whiskey was a treat for the prospective bride's parents. Many of the men would be old enough to be the girl's father.

At that time it was not unusual to have four or five daughters of marrying age in one family to choose from. Whether or not the girls had their eye on another beforehand or in some cases a secret boyfriend the matchmaker and his client would have to have priority.

There was the positive side as sometimes a girl might end up with some auld fellow with a bit of money and land. That would be seen as a lot better than being left as a spinster. As a spinster she would have to make her living sewing or knitting. The parents were anxious to get rid of the daughters. There wasn't much work and money to go round and marriage would mean that there would be one mouth less to feed.

When an old bachelor made his pick of the daughters all that needed to be done was to settle on a bargain. The bachelor would want a sum of money or maybe it might be a cow or two for the privilege of relieving the parents of their daughter. The matchmaker was the middle man and meditator in the deal. When the deal was over, out would come the whiskey, they would drink each other's health, the health of the bride and then they would go.

There was a story of a man who went with a matchmaker and while initially he was keen, during the transactions he made it obvious he had no further interest. Later the matchmaker asked him what went wrong. "Oh" he said "did you not see that I was only getting the frame". This was reference to the poor dowry. Later the man married a much older woman, she had fifty pounds and at that time it was considered a fortune.

Inevitably the girls rebelled. They would go to dances and then runaway with their boyfriends. A woman also had to be very cunning at times to catch her man. Mary Sheridan used to sit at the window of her little cabin looking across at Carrick Mountain and look out at two late burning lights about half a mile away down in the hamlet of Carrick Street. She knew these two lights late on a Sunday night meant that in two houses, girls of her own age had boyfriends visiting.

Mary was jealous. She had to be seen to be attracting a man so she befriended a local farmhand called McQuaid and she quite plainly made a deal with him. All she wanted was for him to visit her house every Sunday night. That is all she asked and in return she would give him two ounces of tobacco each Sunday night when he left.

The farmhand kept his side of the bargain and could be seen making his way past the houses in the hamlet and up the lane to Mary Sheridan's house. This went on for some time, he got his tobacco, a night's chat with Mary's father, tea and oaten bread by a cosy fireside. Mary eventually married the farmhand and as for the two girls she was jealous of, one did not marry until thirty years later and the other ended up a spinster.

47

Coming home from Mass and especially Evening Devotions was also an occasion for romance. There was a seventeen year old fellow who was holding an odd score in learning to plough, started to court a girl. The consensus amongst the gossiping women was that at the age of seventeen he was too young to be courting. This was perceived as being scandalous and him only learning to plough. So the group of concerned women met in council and one of them was dispatched to tell the fellow's mother.

The fellow's mother kept her son under observation and one evening she detected that preparations for courting were underway. He washed, shaved and polished his boots. His mother followed at a distance with a sally rod under her shawl. Her son walked a couple of miles to rendezvous in secret with his new found love.

Caught in an embrace the mother took out the rod and gave her errant son a few lashes telling him that "this isn't a nice thing for you to be at and you only learning to plough". With the rod in hand, she took her son and made him walk in front of her up the road home. The fellow was so embarrassed that he never looked at a girl in his life again.

One of the longest courtships I knew of, was a couple who met at Primary School. It was a regular occurrence to meet them walking hand in hand on the road. In my time when I knew them they were fairly aged. The courtship never waned and they collected the pension together. They both died in their late seventies never having married.

THE HIRING FAIR

The twelfth of May was the traditional date for the Hiring Fair. The Hiring Fair was another opportunity for romance. The young men would be looking for a day out with the young women and the farmers would be looking for boys and girls. Boys and girls would be seen carrying their bundles. This would be all their earthly possessions, which they would take with them for a six month stint of hard work. They were only paid at the end of the six months provided they served the full term.

When a farmer hired a person he would take their bundle just in case the hired help changed his or her mind before the day was out. However the cute ones took two bundles, a dummy parcel and a real one. The dummy parcel was handed over first and if they got a better offer or for any other reason wished to change their mind they could do so without losing their belongings. The most common reason for a change of mind was to be hired by a farmer who would allow them to keep in the company of a new found love.

After being hired at the hiring fair the boy or girl may have to walk or trot several miles behind the farmer's pony and trap or cart. There wasn't any formal induction process to the farm work. A girl would usually have to provide a large pot of potatoes which she boiled for the mens' breakfast at six o' clock the next morning. In the morning she would "teem" the potatoes, that is drain off the boiling water, then empty the pot out onto the centre of a table covered with hempen sack. Butter and salt would be also provided for the dawn meal.

The young men would then go to the barn and flail corn until sunrise. In summer they would go straight to work in the fields. The young women would have to milk the cows. The young men worked to six o' clock in the evening, came in for supper of potatoes and when they were finished they would go back to the barn for another couple of hours with the flail. For six months of this labour a man was paid six pounds whilst a woman was paid five pounds.

AROUND THE FIRESIDE

The heartbeat of the community was in a large country kitchen with a flagstone floor, a large blazing hearth fire of black turf, bleached white pine chairs set in two semi circles behind each other. The crowd would gather for an evening of storytelling and crack. It was an opportunity for the courting couples to meet and for various little competitions to emerge from this social gathering.

When you 'ceilied' with a neighbour the seating arrangement had a regular pattern. The man of the house would sit beside the hearth fire to the front of the house. His wife would be at the otherside of the hearth to the back of the house. The centre in front of the fire was reserved for 'the ceilier'.

One unspoken competition was amongst the pipe smokers. A smoker in the front row would rinse his mouth and would rotate his cheek muscles and spurt out a powerful spit hitting the brown ash at the ring of the fire, sending a small cloud of dust in its wake. A fellow smoker would show off his ability by sending his spit to precisely the same spot. The experts usually took up position in the second row and sent their spit whizzing past their competitor's ear and hit the commonly understood target. The elite spitters could douse

50

a small candle size flame from a blazing turf from the second row.

At that time it was just as important to keep up certain public appearances such as the skill in setting potatoes. On long winter nights local standards would come up for discussion. There was always local competition. Discussions, observations and criticisms of neighbours added greatly to learning in the community.

There was one man who was setting potatoes in heathery ground. Some sprigs of heather were seen to be peeping out at the broo edges. He had to go along with a spade and trim these edges. If not he would have been a local disgrace. Poor workmanship would often be discussed for years afterwards.

There was a case where a man committed the terrible crime of leaving the stump of a rush bush in the middle of a ridge of potatoes. Even the priest conducting the Station Mass was told about this scandal. Rush bushes were tough customers to deal with when you only had a spade. However, you were not a real man if you could not dispose of one and they certainly should not be left as an eyesore on a neat row of potatoes. Fortunately for this man he was married for if he had not been he may never have got a woman.

Ashes surrounding the hearth fire acted as material for maps and sketches. The tongs were used to scatter the ashes on to the flagstones at the front of the hearth and then the tongs became an architect's pencil or a surveyor's pen. Plans of houses, road maps and maps for drainage of fields would appear in the soft ash.

One time a man who had returned from New York was using a tongs and ashes to map out the various districts of the great city. As he kept drawing and explaining he found himself at an advanced position out on the kitchen floor in

51

order to explain the relative positions of the Bronx and Long Island. The woman of the house who was not too pleased with the ashes scattered around her kitchen floor caught her broom and much to the dismay of the returned Yank swept Long Island and the Bronx back into the hearth.

There was a man called Dan Ferry who lived in the house under the same thatch as mine. His bedroom was next to our kitchen, a good design as our hearth fire kept the damp out of our neighbour's bedroom. Paddy Muldoon used to drop in regularly at night for a chat. He was a fidgety man and he used to sit beside our hearth poking around with the tongs at the back of the fire. His pokings usually increased when he was in full flight about his exploits in Scotland. Through time a hole appeared behind the fire and in the end our neighbour Dan Ferry came in and complained that his bedroom was full of smoke.

The fireside discussions used to be mighty stuff, old men getting angry and sweating, especially over politics. One night the topic was the Boer War. One old fellow commented that the Boers were advancing because they had invented a gun called "The Long Tom". He excitedly added that it could throw some hard clods!

I remember the older men telling me how their fathers would stock up for the winter with a supply of herring. They would set off for the Donegal shore with horses and barrels. I am not certain of the location but Killybegs was mentioned. Each horse brought home two barrels of herring in brine. Oatmeal would also be stored in barrels. They would hold about five hundredweight which was compressed into the barrel with a wooden beetle. Wheatflour was purchased in hundredweight bags. The flour brands at that time were Excelsior and the White Man. One of the bags had a picture of a man standing on top of a mountain with a flag. There was another brand of flour which had a picture of a cow. When the flour was nearly finished in the bag it was not unusual to hear someone say "God the flour will soon be finished, we have it eaten down to the cow's elder (udder)".

I heard many stories from Mick Connolly Senior who lived near Duncannon Fort in Carrick. For over a period of thirty years a story told to me by Mick Connolly Senior was disputed by his son and later his grandson. The Connolly home up until around 1957 had a flagstone floor. One very large flagstone measuring approximately six feet by four feet was located in the centre of the kitchen in front of the hearth. The original flagstone was bigger but a piece had to be cut off to allow it in the door. This additional piece lay as a separate flag on the floor.

Mick Senior had told me that his brother John, who was

53

a stone-cutter had laid the flagstone. John Connolly was also a reputed stepdancer. Mick Connolly Senior had added that there was a hole dug underneath this large flagstone. This was to accommodate a large metal pot which was hung from underneath the flagstone. Inside the pot was a tin can. John Connolly the stone-cutter had done this to help create a unique timing sound when he performed his step dancing.

My story was treated with ridicule by the neighbours including the Connolly family. In 1957 when Michael Connolly, the grandson was getting married he decided to put in a new floor and the flags were lifted. The young Michael came right away for me. Exactly as his grandfather had described to me, there underneath the large flagstone was a well, the remains of the pot and the bar which held it in place. The young man offered me the flagstone to take with me. The flagstone was a mountain stone one inch thick, a fine grain and looked very fragile.

Regrettably four men could not get the flagstone lifted onto a tractor trailer so we decided to break it in half. One of the workmen drilled holes with a crowbar at three inches apart but this failed to crack the stone. We had to drill additional holes before the stone broke.

I would like to add here that there is some evidence of the stonemason John Connolly's work in Langfield Roman Catholic graveyard. The headstone on the Connolly Family Grave number 445 on the map of the graveyard was the work of John Connolly. Not recorded on the map is the headstone on the grave of Beatty on the far Northwest corner of the graveyard, also the work of John Connolly. There is also an engraving of a horse on a plaque six inches square on the corner stone of a barn in what was known as McMenamin's of Cooel, now the homestead of the MacAroe family.

**A rubbing taken from John Connolly's
stone cutting.**

MUSIC AND SONG

At the turn of the century on a two mile stretch of the Glen Road there were four house dances going on simultaneously. About thirty or forty people at each dance and two fiddlers at each dance. One dance boasted four fiddlers, three men and one woman from the same family. House dances were a regular event.

In the Carrick area the two most popular fiddlers were Peter McCanny and his cousin Joe. Peter McCanny was a veteran of World War One. Peter was the best fiddler but Joe could play any musical instrument and he composed and sang songs. Joe used to sing an amusing little song called "The Dolly Barton Hat".

The Sets and Siege of Ennis were danced. Part of the sets included swinging your partner, an activity at times which could be dangerous and sometimes in the small kitchens collisions would occur.

Fiddlers expected to get a glass of whiskey during the night. If the whiskey was not forthcoming the fiddle would get angry and a string would break bringing the dance to a standstill. If that didn't bring whiskey another string would break until the message would eventually sink in.

I picked up a number of songs from my father, Patrick Harpur. His favourite was "An Irishman's Toast". Other songs he used to sing were, "Erin's Lovely Home", "Omagh Jail", "The Gauger" and "The Connaught Emigrant to Holland". In the 1920's people mostly sang rebel songs. One I learned then was "Michael Dwyer". My late brother Johnny used to sing a very old song called " Edinburgh Town".

There were the recognised singers and the others. The others would only have learned a bit of a song but that would be their party piece. The better singers that I remember were Mickey "The Shop" McCanny, Jim McLoughlin and Felix McElholm. All were greatly lamented when they emigrated. One of Felix McElholm's songs went:

> "Down in the flowery garden me and this maid went walking
> Down in the flowery garden me and this maid went talking
> She had a little lap dog she called him little Tony
> And everytime I kissed my love he bit my taglione "

A taglione was another name for a coat.

I remember one old woman around 1920 who sang the song " The Black Velvet Band" which was popularised in the1960's and 70's by various Irish ballad groups. Another woman used to sing the "Rocks of Bawn" and " The Maid of the Sweet Brown Knowe". Part of a song I remember but I don't remember the title went:

> "Just like the ivy on the dear old garden wall

57

Clinging so tightly whatever might befall
Just like the ivy I'll be constant and true
Just like the ivy I'll always cling to you ".

There was a Mrs Gileece who sang "The Bonny Bunch Of Rushes Green" which I learned from her in 1920.

Often men working in the fields or in the bog, working at turf would suddenly burst into a verse of a song. This was an indication I suppose that they were happy at their toil. Learning songs depended on your ability to pick up the words and music of a song by listening to another singer. As a result many songs were learned but a number of fine songs were lost because they were never written down.

Another popular song was " The Bonny Wee Window ". This was the story of the fellow who went to see his girl who was not allowed out. She came to the bonny wee window and they started to kiss through the window. Without warning the girl's mother crept up behind the fellow and came down on his back with a stick. The fellow got his head stuck in the window and ended up going off home with the frame of the window on his head.

In the townland of Carrickastoken about six miles on the northern side of Carrick there were three brothers named Hegarty. They were known to be good singers and had an extensive selection of songs. They could also lilt tunes for a night's dancing. One of their songs was "The Wee Croppy Tailor". This was the story of a man who came home and found the wee tailor with his wife. The man picked up the tailor's scissors and cut off his ears thus giving the name of the wee croppy tailor. One of the Hegarty brothers also composed songs and one night he had a "sing your own song" competition with the other local composer Mickey

"Vickey" McCanny. Hegarty is reputed to have won the contest by singing 58 songs to McCanny's 57.

FESTIVE OCCASIONS

At Easter time all the children used to build an Easter house or hut. This was usually constructed with walls of sods. Sticks laid across them and more sods laid on the sticks to form the roof. The highlight for the children was to light a fire in the hut and boil and eat eggs in their special abode on Easter Sunday.

There was a man called Tom O'Kane who was born in Carrick. As a young boy himself and another lad used to mind cattle and horses on Carrick Mountain. They used to catch any loose horses and have a spin on them to break the monotony of minding the cattle. When Easter came they built their Easter house about a mile up Carrick Mountain.

When O'Kane grew up he left Carrick and went to work near Drumquin and then emigrated to America. He made enough money to come back to Drumquin and bought a farm. He farmed there until he was an old man. I remember him arriving in Carrick one Sunday afternoon in a pony and trap. He went up Carrick Mountain to see the remains of his little Easter house which he had built sixty years ago.

Preparations for Bonfire Night the eve of The Feast of St. John The Baptist on the 23rd of June, began with a couple of cartloads of turf. These were emptied beside a nice flat green area. This was usually located on top of a hill. Then a large dyke of heather was made to circumvent the turf at a distance of ten yards. Between one hundred and two hundred people would arrive for the bonfire and dance.

The fiddlers would be there and the young people would dance on the flat green area. The older people and children would sit on the heather. Children used to count how many bonfires they could see on neighbouring hills and identify their precise location. At the end of the night the heather was thrown on to the bonfire and the flames would shoot high into the night sky. This would act as a signal to neighbouring bonfires to do likewise and one could watch the chain reaction of burning of the heather up and down the Glen. Bonfire Night was celebrated in Carrick up until 1963.

Halloween was a time of potato pudding usually called Purty Pudding. Then there was the gathering of apples and nuts. The children around Carrick would set off with their little hemp sacks to gather hazel nuts in Cooel Wood about two and a half miles down the Glen. Cooel Wood at that time covered about twenty five acres. The nuts were brought home and dried by the hearth fire.

One of the games the children played was to select two nuts and name them after a brother and a possible girlfriend or a sister and a possible boyfriend. They then put the two nuts at the edge of the fire and set them alight. If the two burnt brightly together it meant they would have a good life together. If one went out that meant that particular partner would die first.

Other games were biting the apple suspended from the ceiling with a string with your hands tied behind your back. Ducking for apples and sixpences in basins of water was another favourite. Of course ghost stories were told and the parents knew that even if the children were frightened it proved a good deterrent in keeping them in the house on other nights.

Another game played at Halloween was Queen Bee. A

person who was unfortunate enough not to know how the game was played was selected as the queen bee. The queen bee sat buzzing on a chair in the middle of the kitchen while everyone else buzzed off to gather honey. Honey was a mouthful of water. Returning bees buzzed around the queen bee and then in unison showered the queen with the water.

A game played by the menfolk was pulling the stick. This sometimes resulted in a man hurting his back. Two men sat on a floor opposite each other pressing the soles of their feet against each other. Each had a short strong stick. Catching both ends they interlocked their sticks with each other. The competition was then to see which man could pull the other up into a standing position.

I remember one old woman telling me that when she was a young girl, a Halloween custom was that if a girl ate a cooked herring, bones, head, tail and all, she would dream that night of the man she would marry. In her case her dream came true.

At Christmas time the house was decorated with holly. Goose or chicken was the main meal. People used to kill chickens and prepare them for cooking. These were then parcelled up and sent to relations in Scotland or England. The returned gift from across the water would be a fruit cake, sweets or a box of chocolates, a rare commodity at that time.

The Christmas Mummers did their rounds of the houses between Halloween and Christmas. Every house in every townland was visited and culminated in a Mummer's dance just before Christmas. The Mummers were a group of men who acted out a mini drama in the kitchen of your home. The money they collected was to fund the social and dance just before Christmas.

As Mummers usually consisted of the nationalist population they came under great suspicion from the RUC and B Specials. The Mummers being in disguise were suspected of concealing republican activists and in the early fifties during an IRA campaign the Mummers were banned.

Every troupe had a Granny whose job was to provide sustenence for the actors. He was dressed up in a long black dress and white lace cap. Every household knew this and would hide their bread but a good Granny would snuff it out. "Grannys" were known to take scones of bread out of the oven when it was baking over the fire. If the Mummers arrived at the house and the lights were deliberately put out or they were refused entry they would go away from the house making loud wails. A more detailed description of the Christmas Mummers is recorded in a booklet produced by Drumquin Youth Centre, "Drumquin - You're All The World To Me", 1982.

OTHER PASTIMES

Card games were played for halfpennies and if anyone changed a shilling at a card game it would be the talk of the townland for a week. If anyone sought the change of a pound this was exceptionally terrible for no one would have the change of a pound. Another pastime was pitching halfpennies.

Athletic endeavours was another form of entertainment. Pat Ferry was a local man who was quite an athlete. His exploits were related to me by his nephew in 1932 who was then a very old man. So Pat Ferry was probably in his prime around the turn of the century.

There was a story regarding Pat Ferry's prowess concerning a local wedding. A Master McCrea a native of Mountjoy near Omagh was the Schoolmaster in Loughmulhern School. He was getting married to a daughter of the stonecutter Meehan who lived one hundred yards west of Loughmulhern School. It was not unusual that the high spirits of a wedding would cause the young and not so young men to race against horses and cars coming from the chapel.

The bride and groom emerged from St. Patrick's Catholic Church, Langfield and Pat Ferry challenged to race the horse and car the five miles home. Ferry just managed to be ahead on the level part of the road but gained advantage on the steep hills as he came up the Glen. In the end Ferry arrived first at Meehan's house, went in and poured two glasses of whiskey. He was on the steps which led up to the house in time to greet the bride and groom when they arrived.

This topic calls to mind a great folk hero talked about by the storytellers in my youth. There was a man called "Supple Corrigan" who was a great athlete. Whatever crime he had committed he was to be executed. His executioners decided that with this athlete they would have some sport. They decided to let him run cross country and they would run him down with their horses and trample him to death. The race began in Baronscourt near Newtownstewart, County Tyrone. Corrigan kept ahead of the horses for twenty four miles until he reached the village of Kesh in County Fermanagh. There he jumped the river Erne and sat down on the opposite bank. The horses refused to cross the river. Corrigan's chasers are reported to have called over to

Corrigan that he had performed a great jump. Corrigan's reply is supposed to have been "I had a damn good run at it".

The game of "Duck" was popular amongst the men of the area. This was played in the long clear evenings usually on a Sunday. A large stone about twenty five pounds weight was placed in the middle of the road with a small stone the size of your fist sitting on top of it. One man stood near the target whilst his competitor stood about ten feet away. The competitor's job was to lob a forty pound boulder towards the target and send the small top stone flying as far as possible. The man in the middle had to retrieve the stone and replace it before he could "tag" the thrower. If the man in the middle succeeded in tagging the thrower before he reached the spectator group about twenty feet away the thrower had to be "duck in the middle".

Another game played in houses was called " Stick the Links". The competitor was given a short stick and then spun around four or five times in the middle of the kitchen floor until he was a bit dizzy. The competitor had then to run and put the stick through the middle link on the crook chain beside the fire.

Paddy Ferry who lived beside me in Carrick Street taught me a childrens' rhyme which was performed regularly in the townland. This was usually performed by a grandfather or granny on their grandchildren. The granny would have the child standing in front of her and tapping the flat of her hands in alternating rhythmic motions would chant the following rhyme.

"Hurley burley trumpy trace,
The cow has wrecked the marketplace,
A mirley muck, a marley mint,
How many horns stand up?".

She would then raise a number of fingers to indicate a supposed number of horns. The child had to guess the number. If the child got it wrong the exercise continued with the rhyme,

"Two you said and four it was,
Now you get another swizz,
A mirely muck, a marley mint,
How many horns stand up?".

This continued sometimes varying the numbers until the child guessed the correct number which ended in rhyme, e.g.

"Five you said and five it was,
Now you get no more swizz".

This activity was greatly enjoyed by the children although some parents were afraid that an adult might slap their hands too heavily on the childrens back and there was a great fear of "collapsing a lung".

There was another rhyme I picked up from Paddy Ferry which had traces of the Irish language. Some of the words may have been mispronounced so I will describe it as it was passed on to me.

"When I was a wee boy, my petticoat was red
I went out to the world to earn my bread
My auld parents, would rather see me dead
Caw doodle um mavourneen slán
(Codail Mo Mhuírnín Slán)

Chorus

Zoo a zoo a zoo a mul agradh
Sucre an ary sucre an ary croin,
Croin to my aday, daunt to my sucre an ary
Caw doodle um mavourneen slan.

I saddled my horse with a blackhawthorn
With a bridle on his tail and the saddle on his horn,
And oft I went right in the morn
Caw doodle um mavourneen slan.

Chorus

Oh I'll go to the top of yon hill,
And I'll sit down and cry my fill,
And every salt tear will turn a mill,
Caw doodle um mavourneen slan.

Chorus

CHAPTER FIVE

Characters of the area

Despite the hard work, long hours and poor living conditions individual personalities livened up the long dreary nights and the topic of many daily conversations. The storytellers, the pranksters and some people's odd ways, droll humour identified the personalities that had a special role in the life of the locality. There are a number of men and women who stand out in my memory. Most for their humour, others for their trials of life and some which were part of my education for life.

Mickey "Vickey" McCanny (Micí Mhicí)

One such character was a man called Mickey "Vicky" McCanny. Mickey "Vicky" McCanny didn't like being called "Vicky" because this was a nickname.

Mickey was reared by his uncle in the townland of Mullinamac. The remaining stone walls and gables of his little cabin are situated about a mile up the Mullinamac Road from the Glen Road at Carrickbwee. The little house is on the right hand side opposite a sheep dipping pen. The house had a gable end facing the road whilst the other gable was etched into the high bank of heather and moss. The chimney was next to this high bank a few feet below the level of ground.

The position of this chimney was a cause of some fright to Mickey when he was an older man. There had been a very heavy snowfall and a man taking a short cut across the Clunahill mountain accidentally slipped and his feet came down the chimney of Mickey's house. Mickey did not perceive the intruder to be Santa Claus but more likely the Devil himself as Mickey was scared of devils and ghosts.

Mickey's uncle did not treat him well. Mickey left school, as he described himself, when he reached the third book. This was probably at the age of nine years. I am not sure what age Mickey was when his uncle committed him to the Tyrone & Fermanagh Mental Hospital. One of the tests Mickey was set, was to shovel a large pile of sand over a wall next to the Hospital Laundry. He was given a shovel with a rubber handle. Mickey quickly discarded the shovel and found a spade. When his testers arrived they found that the pile of sand was now on the roof of the laundry. Mickey returned home that evening.

Mickey grew to about six feet tall and he spoke with a strong clear voice. He was a big broad reddish faced man. His chest stuck out and he always seemed to be looking out over his chest. He was very excitable and short-tempered. He had a great memory and could talk on any subject and had a great knowledge of world geography.

Mickey was a serious person. He would get up and leave a house if he felt he wasn't being taken seriously. When he was singing no one dare laugh, giggle or talk, otherwise he got very angry. Mickey had a bald spot on his head and when this spot got red he was very angry indeed.

I used to go with him on his Ceilis (visits) to houses. I remember one night Mickey was coming to ceili with a man called Dan Ferry. He overtook Paddy Donnelly. Paddy was an excitable person, not knowing what was the proper thing to say at a particular time. Mickey and Paddy went in to Dan Ferry's house. Everyone in the house greeted Mickey by name just to make sure he knew he was welcome but they forgot about Paddy Donnelly. Paddy was in a fluster so he felt the proper thing to do was to greet Mickey as well. "Well" says Mickey ,"this is the horribilist thing I have ever heard. Walking up the road with a man to Dan Ferry's house and turning around when I went in the door and asking me how are you Mickey".

Mickey was also a strong man. Tests of strength were often performed in farmyards at dinner time when the horses were loosened. Mickey could lift a horse plough with this teeth or two turf barrows with his teeth. On a challenge one day he proved he could pull a plough as good as two horses. He caught the swingle-tree of the plough whilst another man held the plough and he turned a score the length of a field.

The first time I met Mickey was in 1921, I was eight years of age. He had returned after many years working in Scotland. His eyesight was failing. He lived and worked for a man called Eoin McCanny of Cornashesk and also worked a few days a week for my foster mother Catherine Darcy. Catherine used to hire Mickey for three days each week from Candlemas to May to set spuds. During that time he would work in about three roods. Another three roods had to be dug and got ready for corn.

I enjoyed Mickey talking. Out working in the fields Mickey would get involved in some topic or other. He would stand with his arms outstretched, his forehead sweating, his face flushed a purplish red describing some place or incident in vivid detail. A lot of locals regarded him as an eejit. He told me about the Annals of the Four Masters and their references to the exploits of the O'Neills, Earls of Tyrone and Maguire of Fermanagh, some of which took place around the Carrick area.

Later Mickey moved to a house owned by the Carrolls in the townland of Carradowa who provided him with a room of his own. A neighbour of the Carrolls called Armstrong built him a small house on the opposite hillside. Mickey didn't rest there. He moved first to the townland of Kirlish near Drumquin and finally to stay and die in the house of Susan Nugent in the townland of Dressogue about four miles on the Omagh side of Drumquin.

Susan Nugent an elderly lady had three or four other old men who stayed with her, a sort of old folk's home. Susan was once heard to complain about these old men spending all their time around the house during winter. However Susan's description of the problem was "I have three of four old men lying up on me all winter! "

Mickey on one occasion was employed to set spuds along with his employer and another man. It so happened that the order in which they were digging left Mickey with his back to the road. Frank 'Andrew' McCanny came along and noticed this. Now Frank was a bit of a leg-puller. Frank met Mickey later that night and decided to tease Mickey who always took things seriously. Says Frank " I wouldn't let thon boy carry on like I seen today". "What do you mean?" was Mickey's curt response. " He is keeping you working with your back to the road", ventured Frank. "I asked your man about it and he said your face was not too good-looking so he thought it better if he kept your back to the road". The next day Mickey collected his money and left.

Frank McCanny asked Mickey one day to work for him in the bog. "I can't" said Mickey "I have to go to a man called Maguire to help plant spuds." At that time it was the practice to plant cabbage plants in the same ridge as the spuds. The cabbage plants were dropped on top of the manure spread on the ridge for the planter to place a sod on the cabbage plant as he went along. Mickey was short sighted and he would accidently cut the cabbage plants with the spade. As a result he detested cabbage plants. So knowing this McCanny told Mickey "sure I might have known you are going to work for Maguire, sure I have seen Maguire go up the road this morning with a bag of cabbage plants." "He can keep his bloody cabbage plants" snorted Mickey, " I'll go with you for the day."

In the 1920's Tommy 'George' Russell was a special friend of Mickey "Vicky". Tommy Russell was a man who could sing and accompany himself on the violin. Tommy had a brother who also loved music and the violin. So much so that when he was dying he asked Tommy to take down the fiddle and play his favourite tune " Away she goes" as he departed this life.

Tommy and Mickey "Vicky" used to visit each other even though they lived six miles apart and had to walk twelve miles for a night's ceili. One night Tommy visited Mickey and he was afraid to go home late at night. Mickey and Tommy were both terrified of ghosts. So Mickey conveyed Tommy half way home but Tommy was still afraid to go any further on his own and Mickey was too afraid to return on his own. So both men sat down in the ditch by the roadside and sang songs to keep the ghosts away. When daylight came they returned to their homes.

Mickey would make predictions about world events. He would give logical explanations for his pronouncements. Eventually Mickey would weave futuristic calculations into verse. In the 1930's Mickey "Vicky" McCanny told me I would live to see the day when I could take my breakfast in Ireland and be in New York for my dinner. In 1939 he

71

predicted that Germany could not win the war because she was essentially land locked. Her navy was too small and she hadn't enough money to fight. He accurately predicted the USA would enter the War.

Mickey composed songs about burning limestone, grading of the eggs, sinking of wells and any other local, national or international topic of the time. In 1921 Mickey gave me two pennies to buy a copy book from Loughmulhern School and I wrote down a song for him. Mickey's song was about a man called Mr. Daly an agricultural inspector who visited Loughmulhern School.

The following are some lines from that song:

"On the 14th of November as you may understand
A lecture was held in Carrick School by an expert on the land
To show the farmers how to dig and also let them know
The class of seed they were to use and when and where to sow
From each district surrounding, the wealthy farmers came
To listen to the expert, his views and plans explain
Then well contented, went their way, each to his peaceful home
Each man with a plan to work his land, be it either moss or loam
The lecture was a grand success from every point of view
No doubt that Mr. Daly did all a man could do
But the task it is impossible and beyond our earthly lore
For old opinions still hold fast and will forever more
But you'll find the country greatly changed and wonder at the same
As you motor down towards Proughlish town to board an

outgoing train
For a splendid railway station in Proughlish there will be
A regular market of commerce from the centre to the sea
Where Cooel Wood is now standing there will be fertile soil
When man and boy will vie with joy at the fruits of honest
toil
And the ironworks of Carrick will send forth a sullen roar
That will scare the grouse off Tappaghan and the ducks at
Frankie Mor's
And the farmyard at Gorman's, will be a curious sight
Well worthy of a visit then by either day or night
And a gentleman will show them around and its uses will
explain
And hope they have enjoyed themselves and tell them call
again
And the rattle of the motor plough will raise those quiet hills
From Turner's hollow to Wood's Height around by
McEnhill's
And the farmers will be happy then and singing with
delight
As the battery grid at Tom Muldoon's will throw electric
light
To show them how to farm and lengthen out the day
If you have to look for idlers then you will have to use x-
rays."

There was a wee man called Joe McCanny. He was a
forthright individual. He went to work for Father Kelly the
local parish priest of Langfield of the time. He worked on
the small farm and tidying the parochial house. He used to
transport Father Kelly around in a horse and trap and
generally was the priest's righthand man.

Confirmation time arrived and at that time the Bishop stayed over night in the parochial house. Father Kelly gave Joe instructions to wake everyone at seven o'clock in the morning. "Now Joe" said Father Kelly "in the morning tiptoe lightly along the corridor and gently tap on the bishop's door. When the bishop answers, announce that you are "the boy of the house coming to waken you my lord".

The next morning Joe was ready and when the clock struck seven o'clock he sprinted along the corridor as Joe never walked slowly. He gave the bishop's door a kick. "What's, what's wrong" shouted an alarmed bishop. Joe replied, "I'm the lord of the house and I have to come to waken you my boy."

Another story about Joe McCanny concerned a Yankie woman whom he met at a dance. She was wearing perfume, something that was regarded as being quite unusual because only rich women could afford perfume. The smart lads thought that they would put Joe up to leaving the Yankie woman home from the dance. Joe just went in and asked her and she accepted. The next night the smart lads met up with Joe and enquired how he got on with the perfumed Yankie. "Oh very well" said Joe " a lovely woman and there was the loveliest smell off her".

Joe and a few friends one night went in to a country pub near Ederny in County Fermanagh. After drinking a number of pints and being slightly intoxicated, nature called. Joe and his companion went to the outside toilet which at that time was a wide open field. Close by was a spout draining water from a hillside stream which provided a constant flow of water splashing into a tub below.

Joe's friends finished their errand and returned to the

pub. After a while they noticed that Joe had not returned. When they went out again they found Joe standing at the same spot near the water tub. "What's wrong Joe" they asked. In a very sad voice Joe replied "sure I can't get stopped".

At that time when people went to the seaside to bathe they had no swim suits, togs or bikinis. They would undress in the guesthouse or hotel and put an overcoat around them and wade in the sea water. Odd modes of dress reminds me of a man who in the hot summer days would only wear his longjohns. So one day he went into the local village. The police stopped him and were going to charge him with indecent exposure but let him off with a warning and sent him home. So the next day he came into the village this time with the longjohns turned back to front. The police intervened again and reminded him that he had been warned and not to dress that way again. However our friend in the longjohns was quick to point out that he wasn't dressed the same way. "Can't you see I have turned them back to front." The police decided that he had made a fair point and let him go.

Another man who was regarded as an eccentric was the first man to produce silage in the area, fifty years ahead of silage making being introduced to farming. He dug a big hole near the foot of the mountain and piled in freshly cut grass. In the winter time it was from that he fed his cattle.

There was a man called Peter "Kilmore" McCanny. At seventy years of age he used to go to dances and ceilis using the shortest country routes possible. He could be seen jumping low hedges and drains and making his way through the fields. One day Peter was returning from Mass along with a man who lived near Carrick called Paddy McViegh.

Now Paddy McViegh was a drole character. Peter said to Paddy, "the spuds are very poor up our area this year, there is only a top here and top there." McViegh's drole response was " up our way there is only a top here and none there."

Eugene was a shy and innocent man. It was because of Eugene's quiet and innocent ways that humourous stories were attached to him. One time Eugene's wife Mary Anne was sick and was visited by the doctor. Eugene came into the bedroom after the doctor had finished the examination of Mary Anne. Now when Mary Anne had got undressed for bed she had put her skirt over the top of the clock sitting on a dressing table in the bedroom. As the doctor was leaving the bedroom he turned to Eugene and asked him what time it was. In this type of situation Eugene got flustered and turned excitedly to his wife and said "Mary Anne will you ever lift up your skirt there and let the doctor see what time it is."

Eugene had a little mare whom he thought the world of. On one occasion when the mare was in foal he was in the village of Drumquin purchasing some provisions. All the young lads of the village used to think it great sport to tease Eugene. That particular day they started to poke the little mare with sticks and straws. Eugene got very annoyed and went up to the police barracks.

He knocked on the door and the sergeant's wife opened the door and she explained that the sergeant was not in. So Eugene decided to share his plight with the sergeant's wife. "Now Mrs. Sergeant " said Eugene " how would you like to be in foal and have all the young lads of the town tickling your belly with straws and pushing sticks up your ass. Now I don't think you would like it one bit, Mrs. Sergeant."

Early one morning Eugene arrived at a neighbouring

homestead with his little mare. The woman of the house appeared from out behind one of the barns. As fate would have it Eugene's mare began to urinate. Eugene being embarrassed at this happening attempted to chastise the mare. However the statement came out as "Good morning Mrs " and without hesitating turned to the mare and said " didn't you go a long way to pish". It was probably by coincidence that the women was returning from her open air toilet which further aggravated the situation.

One day a pensions officer, whose job it was to ensure people received their old age pension, met Tommy Russell. He asked Tommy the directions to the house of a man that Tommy did not like. "I'll tell you something" said Tommy "when that fellow was a baby his mother went out and forgot to leave the tongs across the cradle. The fairies came and left nig the boy (the devils child) instead"

Hugh Gallogly was another man for humorous remarks. Late July was the time to load the rucks or ricks of hay in the meadows on to the horsedrawn carts. These were brought to a sheltered spot near the farmhouse known as the haggard and built into a large haystack. A familiar sound then would be the creaking of cart axles and the clanking of the metal rims on the cart wheels on the stony roads and lanes. It would be the occasion of much pride for a farmer bringing home his hard-won hay and every man prided the quality of his own hay.

There would be a great hive of activity with a couple of men on carts drawing the hay to the haggard, two loaders in the meadow and two men with pitchforks lifting clouds of hay to two or maybe three builders on a stack. Another man would be hand-pulling untidy ends of hay from the sides of the stack as it gradually rose to overshadow the cow byres.

Hugh Gallogly was observing all the to-ing and fro-ing of the hay carts, as he lived on the side of a lane which led to a neighbouring farmer's house. Hugh wandered up to the scene of the sweating men and dusty hay being flung skywards to the haystack. "Well" said the proud farmer " what do you think of that hay Hugh, great stuff is it not?". It had been a wet summer and when hay is put into rucks in a dampish state the centre of the ruck would go through a natural chemical process and would heat and steam at the heart. This was a telltale sign of poor harvesting skills. Hugh was the drole sort. Placing both hands on his hips and looking thoughtfully into the distance as if to consult the blue peaks of Donegal peeping through the late summer haze, Hugh gave his considered opinion. "I was watching my brother Pat take a handful of hay from one of the carts as it passed and he dropped it very quickly and stuck his fingers in his mouth." Hugh was joking of course but this would be the sort of crack the fellows in the haggard would enjoy.

Hugh was once asked to give his views on a local fiddler. A caustic critic he was. "Well to tell you the truth" said Hugh "that man's fiddling reminds me of a man sharpening a saw." Hugh told the story of his nephew Dan, a tall dark man in his thirties who had a great passion for fiddling. "He came in here the other night and sat at the hearth and fiddled and puffed and stamped his feet till he sent the splanks (sparks) flying up the chimney. So I went out to the byre and sat on the milking stool and smoked my pipe. In the rear I came in again after about two hours when the last splank had gone up the chimney."

There was a man who lived near Drumquin called Moore who insisted on walking everywhere and would not use a horse, bicycle or motor car. He once walked to Derry city forty miles away to buy a sixteen-pound sledge hammer. He would refuse lifts from motor cars explaining that he was in a hurry.

There was a man called Carroll who returned home after many years working in the U.S.A. He claimed that if one worked as hard in Ireland as they did in America and did some economising they would be just as well off. The Yankie Carroll walked four miles one day to the local store which adjoined the old creamery near Drumquin to buy a shovel. A fellow customer told him that shovels were a penny cheaper in Omagh. So Carroll walked a further eight miles to Omagh. Carroll returned to America after two years.

There was a man called Johnnie Livingstone, locals pronounced his name Leevison. Johnnie was a caretaker for the Church of Ireland which was located in the townland of Drumrawn near Drumquin. Johnnie hired a little man called Jimmy Wilson to mow the graveyard. The little man had the strange knack of pushing the sned of the scythe with his knee when he was mowing but nevertheless was considered an expert mower.

When Jimmy arrived to mow the one and a half acres he was confronted with an abundance of great tall thistles. When the caretaker arrived Jimmy had finished the job but had left all the thistles standing. The caretaker asked him why he left the thistles. Jimmy's response was that he had only been hired to cut the grass. Of course Jimmy's real reason was to show off his talents as a mower.

Jimmy Wilson was also known for his quick wit. One example was when Jimmy was doing odd jobs around the house for the local doctor. The doctor hadn't really much work for Jimmy but asked him to plaster a wall. Now Jimmy was no plasterer. When the doctor arrived on the scene there was mortar scattered everywhere and Jimmy was trying to level out the plaster with a trowel.

"I see the trowel covers a lot of mistakes" teased the doctor. "Aye" said Jimmy "and the spade and shovel covers a lot of yours".

On another occasion Jimmy got drunk and the local police sergeant took him into the barracks to sober him up a bit before sending him home. The sergeant had Jimmy in the dayroom when the sergeant's children ran in. "Keep those youngsters away from me" screamed Jimmy. "Why" said the sergeant. "All our ones at home have got the fever" said Jimmy. The sergeant couldn't get Jimmy out of the barracks fast enough.

My foster father Barney Darcy had a brother called Mick. A strong man was Mick. He agreed to work a day at flailing corn for a landlord called Patterson who lived in the townland called Cooel. Patterson agreed that the payment for the day's work was for Mick to carry home as much straw as he could carry. Mick worked hard all day in the barn loft flailing the corn and throwing down the straw to the floor below.

By nightfall Mick had threshed about a horseload of straw. With the help of other farmhands they tied a rope around the load and lifted it onto Mick's back. Mick was just leaving when he met Patterson. The landlord felt that Mick had got the better share of the bargain. After a heated exchange Mick carried the load back and unloaded half of it and carried his half home.

On another occasion Mick went into the village of Drumquin and consumed a little too much drink. The sergeant and two policemen tried to arrest him. Mick was having none of it. He knocked them about and took the belts off the three policemen and threw them up on the roof of a house. Mick was later summonsed and fined. He had no money to pay the fine and was facing the possibility of imprisonment. He had some hay which he had tried unsuccessfully to sell in order to raise the money.

However in time he got a most surprising buyer, the police sergeant. It was the sergeant's way of saying how he respected Mick's physical strength. Interestingly Mick went to Scotland and became a policeman. He had a reputation there for being able to handle himself and deal with the rough and tough. However in the end Mick got what proved to be a fatal blow from a brick and died in a Glasgow hospital.

Tom Connolly lived in Carrick Street. When Tom was a young married man he was noted for his fine head of golden curls. One day Tom went to the local village. He promised his wife Sally that he would be on his best behaviour. Tom returned home and speaking very properly and maintaining an obviously erect posture he informed his young wife. "Sally-I-had-only-one-drink-today". Sally said that that was fine and put a big bowl of soup in front of Tom. Tom continued to assure Sally that everything was just fine as he had only had one drink. Sally slipped down to the bedroom. After about ten minutes she returned to a not surprising scene. Tom was fast asleep with his head and his lovely curls in the bowl of soup.

Francie "Neilly" McCanny was a bachelor who lived with his sister. Francie was reasonably well off, had a fine house and a fair sized farm. He was a powerfully built man. He was capable of lifting a two hundred-weight bag of grain over the side of a cart with a shovel. On one occasion he came across a car which had driven into a drain on the roadside. Francie went to the front of the car and lifted it out onto the road. Then he went to the rear of the car. The driver of the car intervened and asked Francie to wait until he got the passengers out. "Never mind" said Francie and lifted the rear of the car out onto the road too.

One day Francie went to the village of Ederny. He had a drink and felt like a bit of sport. So Francie decided to visit Maguire's hardware shop. "Mrs. Maguire I have no bed. My wife has to lie on the sofa and I lie on the horse's collar in the loft." He also asked Mrs. Maguire for scrap pieces of hardboard which he told her he would use as half-soles for his shoes because he could not afford leather. Mrs. Maguire didn't know Francie and in future whenever she met anyone from his area she would enquire about this poor man who couldn't afford to mend his shoes and had to sleep on the horse's collar.

A new police sergeant arrived in the village of Drumquin. He prided himself on being a clever detective. His first case was the malicious burning of a peak (large round stack) of hay. The sergeant sought out what he reckoned to be the font of all information in the area, the local postman. So the sergeant approached the postman for help. "Sure I can help you" said the postman "you are looking for likely suspects you say. Well I can give you the names of the culprits parents". The postman gave the sergeant the names of three parents. The sergeant set off to the first house. The man and woman were churning. "Where was your son on such and such a night" enquired the sergeant. The astonished man said " what's wrong with you?" "answer my question" retorted the stern sergeant. The man lost his temper and flew into a rage and was going to hit the sergeant. Eventually the wife intervened to inform the sergeant that they had been married for thirty years and they had no family.

Reckoning that he had made a mistake the sergeant proceeded to the next house. The same question " where was your son on the night of such and such" . This man reacted a little cooler. "Somehow I can't answer your question now". "You will have to answer my question" said the angry sergeant. Here again the wife intervened to say that they had been married nearly thirty years and had no family. A repeated experience at the third house convinced the sergeant that he had been well and truly duped.

Then there was the new constable who came up the Glen on his annual pilgrimage of seeking out unlicenced dogs. Although every house had at least one dog he failed to find any dogs, licienced or otherwise. The constable met a young boy who was in his barefeet. "I will give you half a crown young lad if you can tell me where I can find an unlicenced dog about here". "Well" said the boy "I can show you two". The police constable gave the boy the half crown and asked him to show him the way.

The boy told the constable to follow him. The boy climbed over the ditches and through fields, into marshy ground and up through the mountain. The mud covered constable with water squelching from his boots eagerly followed the boy. Eventually the boy stopped and pointed down to a deep bog hole. Two dogs had been drowned there. "There's your two unlicenced dogs constable" shouted the young boy as he took off and ran with his half crown across the mountain.

The three Figgerty brothers lived near Carrickistokan. They distilled very good poteen. Understandably they were very secretive about their operations and no one got access to the still. The police tried all sorts of approaches but without success. Then one day a new constable arrived in Drumquin. He went secretly to one of the Figgerty's and asked him for a half pint of poteen. He assured Figgerty that this was for personal use and he would not report him. Figgerty said that was fine and agreed to meet him at an agreed rendezvous. Figgerty arrived as agreed and handed over a bottle. "Right" said the constable "you have escaped the law for a long time but I've got you now." "Ye might think that until you have tasted it" said Figgerty. The constable checked and found that it was a bottle of water.

Another time Figgerty had a big consignment of poteen to deliver. It had to go through the village of Drumquin. Figgerty leaked information that he would deliver the poteen packed inside a load of turf on a donkey's cart. There would be two cart loads of turf and the contraband would be in the first cart. The police were waiting, having been briefed by a "reliable" informer. They seized the first cart and took Figgerty and the cart to the barrack's yard. There they unloaded the turf. Meanwhile the second cart passed through and the poteen reached its customers. The sergeant was furious. "Figgerty you watch out, I'm keeping a good eye on you". Figgerty replied " and I am keeping my two eyes on you."

The Figgertys had a little white terrier who was an important agent in the defence of the still. One brother would always be in the house and when the police would be sighted he would just call "police" and the terrier would scurry off into the mountains to alert the brother at the distillery.

The illegal distillation of poteen reminds me of a song, one of the earliest I remember, which summed up the people's dislike of the authorities who hounded them.

I was born one day in a spot called Old Erin,
Where shillelagh and whiskey was plenty they say.
And as I grew older and fond of the lassies,
A happy gay fellow in every spree.

My days and nights I spend jolly and frisky,
Till I fell in love with one Biddy Malone,
Her father distilled and kept good poteen whiskey,
And under the ground he kept fine Inishowen.

Young Biddy herself was not a Venetian Beauty,
You couldn't compare her to Duchess or Queen,
A cousin of Biddys, a north country Carman,
Tried to gain the whip hand, but the fields were too green.

When this gulpin found out that Miss Biddy perferred me,
Straight away to the gauger he instantly went,
Saying now if your honour if you'll kindly reward me,
To turn an informer I am fully bent.

My cousin Biddy she has got a husband,
A lump of an ugly Dublin jackeen,
And this very night we will give them a fright,
For we'll spill all their whiskey right out on the green.

Now I being accustomed to still operations,
I yoked up my horses for three miles around,
Expecting that night that the gauger being on me,
If he didn't come he be sure the next day.

I dug a big hole at the end of my still house,
Quite large enough to hold twelve or thirteen,
I filled it with muck and on top then I stuck,
A few sods of Erin to make it look green.

Early next morning I went to my still house,
Expecting to have a gull in my clutch,
The carman and gauger had sunk to the bottom,
Be sure in my heart I didn't pity them much.

When the carman and gauger had sunk to the bottom,
Not a bit of their carcase was to be seen,
Some they were praying and others hurraying,
For the fate of the auld gauger way down in the green.

An advice I will give to all young fellows courting,
And let it be a warning to every young man,

Don't be too sure of the girl you're in love with,
Perhaps she might have recourse to this plan.

Don't be too sure of the girl you're in love with,
Some awkward fellow might slip in between,
There's many a slip between the cup and the lip,
Like the slip the auld gauger got down in the green.

Another story concerning one of the Figgerty brothers
was when his wife had become ill and required a nurse. The
nurse lived in the townland of Dooish about five miles away.
Figgerty asked the nurse to come and attend to his wife. The
nurse refused as she was elderly and she knew she would
have to walk three miles by road and then a further two
miles up a mountain track to Figgerty's house.

Figgerty promised that if she came to where the mountain
track joined the road he would make it easier for her to get
up the mountain. So the nurse set off walking with
Figgerty and when they came to where the mountain path
joined the road Figgerty produced a creel which was hidden
in the hedge. He strapped the creel to his back and carried

the nurse in the creel to his house. When she had completed her nursing duties Figgerty carried her back to the road again in the creel.

"Red" Frank McCanny was diagnosed by his family as suffering from heart fever. Frank was hot tempered and didn't believe in cures and personally disliked the man who performed the "oatmeal trick", which was the cure for heart fever. Frank had been confined to bed and had been prevailed upon by his family to allow them to send for the "cure". Frank told the story of the visit of the man with the cure. "He stuck his head around the bedroom door, took one look at me and said "just in time! By God if I had a pitchfork I would have stuck it in him"!

Frank's wrath extended to the words of comfort from the priest. Frank was poorly with a chest complaint. The local priest visited him to offer spiritual support. "You know" said the priest "that the more God loves you the more he gives you to suffer." "He must be wild fond of me " said Frank " because He has me nearly killed."

In later years Frank moved from the Carrick area to live in a new council estate in the village of Drumquin. Frank had been a wise farmer and practical in his outlook. He knew that one of the best ways of preparing new ground for grass was to set a crop of potatoes. This he applied to the front lawn of his new home knowing that he would have a year's crop of potatoes and the ground would be well prepared for a fine lawn the following year.

The council rent collector chastised Frank for planting potatoes at the front of his house and was he not aware that he should have planted grass. "God" said Frank " I have no teeth left to graze with."

There was the story of a woman who lived on the

Mullinamac Road. She had put in a garden of spuds. A neighbouring woman seeing her enterprise decided to follow suit but she had no spade. So she borrowed the spade from the woman on the Mullinmac road. The spade was a long time away before the borrower returned it.

When the borrower returned the spade the Mullinamac woman used tact in expressing her annoyance about the delay in returning it. She took out a sally rod that was leaning against the wall of her house. She beat and scolded the spade for being away for so long. After she had chastised the spade she invited her neighbour in for a cup of tea and both parted on friendly terms.

Father Gormley arrived as a curate in the Langfield parish in 1913. He always had a special word for me as I was the first child he had baptised in the parish. Father Gormley was a big stout man with sharpish features and he smoked a pipe. He was very interested in folklore and in every bush and rock in the countryside. He questioned everything.

Before the coming of the motor car a man called Harry McPeake used to drive the priest around on a horse and trap. When a sick call would come Harry who was a bit reluctant to travel awkward routes would ask Father Gormley if there was any real need to go. One wet and stormy night Harry and Father Gormley went out on a sick call. The horse and trap could not make it up a make-shift mountain lane so they left the trap and stabled the horse in a nearby shed. They continued their journy up this long and winding muddy lane, partially overgrown with bushes. A very disheartening journey. At one point Father Gormley said to Harry " do you think we'll make it to this sick man at all?" Harry replied "we're not going to make it, we'll turn and go home and let him go to hell until the morning." However

Father Gormley persevered and reached the sick man.

It was a custom that time that if you were in the company of a man who smoked a pipe and if you knew he was out of tobacco you gave him your ounce of tobacco. Your neighbour would cut off enough to fill his pipe. This was a favour which was regularly exchanged. One day Father Gormley went to visit a man who lived up near Carrick, for a day's shooting of rabbits and wild fowl. The man brought the priest into his house gave him tay and generally made him welcome.

The two men went out to the mountain and Father Gormley decided to stop and have a smoke. He took out a two ounce block of tobacco and filled his pipe. He then handed his companion the tobacco so he could fill his pipe. His companion filled his pipe and much to the consternation of the priest he put the remainder of the tobacco in his pocket.

Father Gormley wondered how he would get his tobacco returned. So later he took out his pipe and felt around about his pockets and said to the man " I could have sworn that I had two ounces of tobacco with me and I don't seem to have it now. " The man took out the tobacco and gave it to the priest. After filling his pipe the priest thought it would be nice to offer his companion another fill again. The man again filled his pipe and put the remainder of the tobacco back in his pocket and it was never returned.

Michael McCrea was a bachelor who lived near Loughmulhern School. He was a nephew of Meehan the stonecutter who owned the farm and house before him. Meehan was a good farmer but these skills didn't seem to pass on to his nephew. Michael would not be satisfied that turf were ready enough to bring home so he would wait a little longer. As a result there was often six years "cuttings of turf", left lying on the mountain. He struggled with hay making. If the day was good he would prefer to sit in the sun and then make a mad rush at working at nightfall. His hay would be in the field when everyone else had theirs in their barns.

McCrea had lots of ceiliers. All the young tricksters of the area would visit him. They would enjoy McCrea sitting up in his armchair beside the fire telling serious stories. One night he was recounting his visit to the Drumquin fair to his assembled and hushed audience. He had purchased a wee polly cow (that is one without any horns). He bragged away about this little polly cow. Francie Donnelly a fellow who used to stick out his unusually long tongue when he got excited was sitting behind Michael McCrea. Francie flashed out the big long red tongue like a snake. "Michael" said Francie " are you sure that wee cow had no wee butts of horns at all." The giggles simmered around the house and built up into an uncontrollable burst of laughter. McCrea wasn't pleased.

One night McCrea was out but the crowd gathered as usual. They decided that one of them would act McCrea. The subject of the mini drama was that McCrea would get married. Another fellow acted as McCrea's wife. The wife got sick and they put her to bed. Then she started to moan as if in child labour. Another group of men ran out and pretended to be horses and pulled the cart up and down the road as if going for a doctor. Another acted the part of the doctor and arrived and treated the wife.

One very frosty night when the roads were very slippery. McCrea was away again. The comedy sketch was on again, this time three fellows got on McCrea's bicycle to go for the

91

doctor. The three fellows on the bicycle crashed on the slippery road and wrecked the bicycle. The next night that they gathered in McCrea's he chased them telling them never to return. A few nights later McCrea asked them all back. He had got lonely and missed their company. However the crowd had moved to another location and they never returned.

McCrea was a county councillor. In 1940 he opposed the Glen Road being tarmacadamed. This was because he felt that his mare would slip on the smooth surface. McCrea thought a lot of the mare. He would test the ground in a field ahead of the mare in case it was too hard or too soft going.

The Donnelly family from Carrick at one stage were roadmaking contractors. I remember seeing three hundred yards of coarse boulders piled up six feet high along the roadside at the quarry in the townland of Curragh. A mobile stonebreaker was due to come and break the stones fine enough for use in roadmaking. The breaker didn't come so the Donnelly brothers broke the stones manually. They used four pound sledge hammers and small knapping hammers. Day after day going and coming from school we would see the Donnellys up there on the pile of stones hammering away and slowly the long pile of boulders were converted into large pebbles.

Paddy Donnelly was a very stong man although he was only of medium build. One time he took two hundred weight of artificial manure in a wheelbarrow from the Glen Road up to his house. The path was up the steep gradient of Carrickard, rising to eight hundred feet on which a horse could not climb. This steep incline was named locally as Donnelly's Croft.

Paddy Donnelly chewed tobacco. When Paddy came on

his ceili he would start the night by slipping a square of tobacco into his mouth. During the night as Paddy chewed I used to watch the little bulge on his cheek get smaller and smaller as the night wore on. Paddy died at the age of eighty four.

The Donnellys were also fond of sport but usually they were working too hard to have any leisure time. Boxing was their favourite sport. Paddy and Francie Donnelly used to box on the way home from cutting turf. Paddy was a very direct fighter but Francie used to bob and weave and throw a sneaky punch. Even when they would strike each other hard they could laugh and tease each other over dinner how they made their punches connect.

Francie used to practice sparring, by poking the behind of a flinging mare and trying all sorts of positions in evading the animal's kicks.

Kitty Darcy was a big strong woman. All her family had emigrated and her house was empty. Kitty was hired to a farmer near Drumquin. One day she decided to come home to Carrick. She walked eight miles to Omagh and purchased about four stones of provisions, tea, sugar, flour and meal. This she carried in a bag slung over her shoulder. She walked all of fourteen miles to Carrick. When she arrived in Carrick there was no turf for the fire. She put a creel on her back and climbed Carrick Mountain a mile away and returned with her fuel. Then she made herself tay and sat down and smoked her clay pipe.

Kitty got a little dog from a man named Beatty who lived in the townland of Sanahowen near Lack in County Fermanagh about three miles over Carrick Mountain. Kitty called the dog Beatty and she thought the world of her little dog. One day Kitty was footin' turf on Carrick Mountain. A neighbouring man John Starrs was also footin' his turf about half a mile away. John Starrs was well known for conserving his energy. He wouldn't walk one step out of his way to oblige a neighbour.

That day little Beatty started to stare and barked over in the direction of John Starrs. Kitty began to jump up and down and wave her arms. John was alarmed and hastily made his way through the clumps of heather and wet bog holes to reach Kitty.

When he arrived he said "my God Kitty what's the matter" "it's Beatty" said Kitty "he began to bark over at you thinking you were my nephew Barney, so I just called you over to let Beatty see that you were not Barney."

Roseanne Reid was a local woman who ran her own little farm. She kept cattle and was an efficient farmer, every bit as good as her male contemporaries. Sometimes she would hire a man for the odd day to help her with the farm work. Roseanne could mow a meadow as well as any man but as she advanced in years she had to hire a man to mow.

On one occasion she was watching her hired help mow. She was not impressed. She went into the meadow and proceeded to show him how to adjust his scythe. She was later to remark that she raised him, she lowered him and she proved that he was no man! The raising and lowering of course referred to the settings of the scythe blade.

Roseanne kept fourteen cattle and a bull. She did not drive this herd, they followed her. She stopped they stopped. She cut and won her own turf and could be seen going off to the mountain followed by her herd of cattle. Then the sad day came when Roseanne fell into ill health and died shortly afterwards. She apparently decided that she was not going to die at home. So she decided to walk to Drumquin followed by her herd of cattle. She stopped at Carrick and made her way into Carrick Street and came to my house.

My foster mother Catherine made her tea and some scone bread. She then asked Catherine " do you keep a townhouse?" Catherine did not understand. Roseanne clarified her query "I mean do you keep lodgers?" Roseanne wanted to stay. Catherine couldn't see this as a feasible arrangement and this was reinforced when she could see that the cattle standing on the street would only follow one master, Roseanne. This was the last I saw of poor old Roseanne as she left followed by her faithful cows.

Shortly after the Famine a local widow had a field of corn to cut. She got a neighbouring man to come and cut the corn. She knew that the man had to start the day probably only having a small breakfast. So she waited until he had cut a few bunches of corn. She picked them up, took and flailed the corn. Then she used quirons to grind the oats. Later she brought the tea and oaten bread made from the newly ground oats to the man working in the field.

There was another local woman who could do a man's work and worked alongside men doing heavy physical work. She was known as "Peggy the man". She was small and sturdy. She could match any man mowing fields of hay. Peggy was often seen mowing hay in the large holms (large flat fields) which lay between the Omagh Road in Drumquin and the Fairy Water River. In her spare time Peggy used to mend shoes.

There was the story of a widow woman who kept her cows in the byre all winter without having cleaned it out. As a result a large dung hill or locally called a "doughal" built up inside the byre. The widow hired a small light man called Tommy to clean out the byre. He was a very slow worker. The next day she hired a big strong burly man called John to finish the job. Some days later she told her neighbours about the two men. "Now I had Tommy here and he was a very delicate dunger but John was a good strong dunger."

Mrs. Cassidy lived in the townland of Gortnasole about two and half miles west of Carrick. She died at the age of one hundred and twelve. She never had travelled more than twenty miles from her home.

Mrs. Cassidy as a younger woman worked on the land for a local farmer. Shortly before her death in 1985 she was able to relate how she handed the liners and the bonnets to the men making drains in the fields. This was a reference to the names of the stones used in making drains. She continued her normal housework duties until the year she died.

Molly Mimniagh lived in the townland of Tully north of Carrick. In her spare time she made poteen. The police would come and sieze her still. The police regarded Molly as a " responsible" poteen maker, as she would never give the brew to young people. The police used to leave her still out in the backyard of the police barracks. Next morning the still would be gone and in operation again.

One night a group of young lads arrived at Molly's house looking for a few bottles of her best brew. She told them to sit down and watch her make the brew as it would not be ready for an hour. She also pointed out that she hadn't yet put in "the plump". After an hour she went outside and returned with a shovelful from her dry toilet and added this plump to the brew. Needless to say she lost those customers.

Molly also had stepping stones out into Lough-a-Bradan which only she knew. When chased by police she would take the still on her back and using her secret path would walk out into the water. The police would never venture to wade in. Molly could do a man's work and wore leggings and gaiters. She was mannish looking and locals referred to her as "a muffle bite". I presume they meant an haemorphadite .

In 1947 there was an oldish woman who came from Scotland to live in Carrick. She took up residence in the old school house near Corlishog Bridge. She was a Mrs. Brennan and she ran a little grocery shop. The school children were very fond of her. Mrs. Brennan used to leave a bucket of spring water and a cup in the hallway. This was for the children coming from school during summer days who may be in need of a drink. She loved to hear the news of the country, especially romantic stories, courtships and marriage difficulties. Most of the stories she was told were either false or exaggerated.

There were stories of troubled marriages. One case was a man who lived in the west of Carrick and he married a girl who came from the far side of Drumquin about ten miles away. The man treated his new wife very badly. He made her do all the hard labouring work. When setting potatoes she would have to dig out the trenches to form the ridges whilst he would take the easy job of shovelling up the loose clay. He would not allow her to rest but he would go off for a quiet smoke of his pipe.

The young woman endured this hardship for a few years. Then one day she left and was seen carrying her bags down the Glen Road as she made her way back home to outside Drumquin. The next day the husband went down the Glen Road with a rope over his shoulder. Later that evening he came back with his wife and the rope tied around her neck dragging her back to his home.

There was the story of a big strong woman who married a small frail man and treated him very badly. She would sometimes tell him to go up the mountain for a creel of turf just when he was about to get into bed. Off he had to go wearing only his shirt. This he had to do even in winter time during frost and snow. Perhaps it was an early form of contraception or to cool his passions. It may of course also have been some sort of masochistic sexual ritual.

There was the story of a man who went on his pony and trap to the doctor, his complaint was that he had an upset stomach. He told the doctor that he took bicarbonate of soda to help his stomach. The doctor chastised him for taking soda and told him that it would ruin his stomach. The doctor gave him a bottle which cost the man three pounds and six pence about a day and a half's pay. As the man was going down the laneway from the doctor's house he overheard an interesting dialogue. The doctor came running out and started to yoke up his horse to go on a sick call. The doctor shouted to his wife " Margaret will you get me a glass of water and a spoonful of soda, I'm dying with the heartburn."

To rear two sons and make sure that they had no contact with girls was a task one woman set herself. She wanted her sons proper in every way and succeeded in keeping them isolated from the advances of females until they were forty years of age.

Her protected species eventually became an irresistable challenge to a few of the local girls. They infiltrated the sanctuary of this woman's home by initially showing no interest in her sons. On visits to the house the girls would sit and pull their long skirts up and expose not just an ankle or a calf but a piece of the female anatomy forbidden to the eyes of a single man then, a woman's knee. This put the mother into defensive strategies of having to sit in positions so as to screen and prevent what she called "her two cubs" being violated by these brazen hussies.

Then one day a terrible thing happened. Her two cubs were cutting turf. On the adjacent ground separated by a ditch was a neighbour's daughter. The cubs stopped their work and sat on the ditch and were joined by the neighbour's daughter for a bit of an innocent chat to break the boredom of the work. An eagle-eyed wisecrack spotted the opportunity for a bit of fun. He dropped in to the cubs' mother and related his sightings. The mother jumped up, pulled an old black shawl around her shoulders and firmly stepped it out to the girl's home. The girl's mother was delighted to see her neighbour who had not visited her for years. The cubs' mother got straight to the point. "I just came here to tell you to keep your she-wolf at home." The cubs never married though one of them would break out now and again and chat up a girl. He never got any further as he lived in constant fear of "a gar" that was the local term for a gossip.

99

Mickey Gorman lived in the townland of Garrison Glebe. He was a very intelligent man who read a lot. Unfortunately he spent most of his life hired by cruel landlords. When he was older and partly disabled from his hard life he returned home and spent his time repairing clocks. He could repair any clock except that his hands were too big and clumsy. Mickey compensated by getting children to insert the small cogs and wheels under his instructions.

One evening during a heavy fall of snow Mickey was passing through the village of Lack in County Fermanagh with his horse and cart. The young lads of the village pelted him with snowballs and Mickey was annoyed. He was coming near to the police barracks and he called out for help. The police standing inside the window were amused at Mickey's plight and didn't stir.

A large hard clump of compacted snow that had come from under a horse's hoof landed in the cart. Mickey picked it up and put it under his big overcoat. He then moved the horse and cart forward until he was directly in front of the police barrack windows. From under his coat Mickey let fly the lump of snow, smashing the window of the police barracks. This had the desired result, as the police soon cleared the young lads off the street.

A crow built its nest high up on a tree in Mickey's laneway. Mickey took out the shotgun to shoot the crow but everytime he got near enough for a shot the crow would fly away. He noticed that whenever he was riding the horse under the tree the crow didn't fly off. Mickey saw his chance. He got the gun and got up on the horse and trotted down to the tree. Mickey took aim and fired but the horse bolted and threw Mickey into the hedge.

One day Mickey was building rucks of hay. Mickey was

on the top of the ruck and a man named Harry McCanny was forking up the hay. Now Harry was a trickey customer and played lots of pranks on people. Harry was also renowned for his remarkable eyesight. Most people would see the figure of a man in the distance. Harry could tell you who he was.

That day Harry spotted a man walking through distant fields with a shotgun. Mickey hadn't noticed nor did he notice Harry slipping off to a nearby stream for a handful of gravel. Harry kept forking up hay and chatting to Mickey but all the time watching the man with the gun. When Harry saw the man lift the gun and aim and on the instant of the flash he hit Mickey in the face with the handful of gravel. Mickey fell off the ruck tossing it in the process and shouting and screaming that he had been shot. Mickey took it all in good sport as he did with all the tricks played on him, a reason why he was a very well liked man in the locality.

CHAPTER SIX

Crafts

There were many crafts evident in the community. These ranged from all the skills required in the construction of a house to basket weaving, churning and sewing. House building was a community effort. A house could be built in a day. Starting with the enticement of a couple gallons of whiskey or poteen and food, the men of the locality would gather up and building commenced. The foundations were not very deeply dug unless the ground was soft. The walls were built with two rows of stones leaving a cavity, which the older men and children filled up with baskets of fine stones and clay. Most houses just had a kitchen and one bedroom each measuring fifteen feet square. Everything would operate in a planned fashion. The carpenters would be constructing the couples (trusses) for the roof. These couples would be made from seasoned timber and the horizontal rafter was called a baulk which was secured by wooden dowels to the legs of the couple. The short board which tied the couple together at the top was called the hoof and was also secured by wooden dowels.

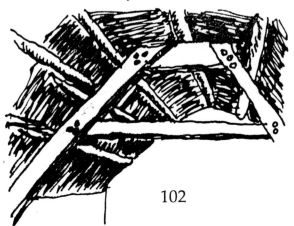

Another expert operation was cutting roof sods or scraws. These had to be cut to run from the fifteen foot long wallplate, over the rigging and down to the opposite side. The scraws had to be one inch thick and were rolled up with a stick through the centre for carrying. Two men holding each end of the stick would roll the scraws clayside inwards on to the roof timbers. This would continue until the roof was completely covered. The second coat of scraws would be laid so as to overlap the joins.

Some men would be cutting rushes with scythes. These rushes which would be dipped in bluestone and would form the thatch. Others would be cutting hazel rods for scollops which held the thatch to the bed of scraws. At that time a thatcher was paid ten pounds for thatching a house. Finally when the flagstone floor was laid the house warming began and the dancing ensured that the floor was firmly put in place.

The fireplace was about five feet wide. The chimney brace started about five to six feet above floor level. This was built on a thick wooden beam suspended by two stone corbels which rested on two pillar-like legs of stone at each side of the fireplace. The corbels were of similar thickness as the legs but stuck out approximately at a forty five degree angle. In earlier times a stick or crook was put across the chimney higher up. A chain was suspended from the crook in which to hang pots and pans over the hearthfire. In later times an iron crane was used. This was a vertical piece of five and a half feet high iron hinged at the left hand side of the fireplace. A horizontal bar was forged at right angles to the top of the vertical. From the horizontal bar hung the chains and crooks for the pots and pans. This crane enabled a couple of pots to be heated at the same time and one could swing the crane outwards for easier and safer removal of hot pots.

Most houses had a variety of black metal pots for boiling potatoes or vegetables. A big frying pan with a basket type handle for hanging on the crook and the griddle for baking oatmeal scones. A household could survive on a pint of parafin oil in a week. This was used for the oil lamps as it was wasteful to use parafin to light the fire. Instead the fire would be raked at night so that the embers would still be alive in the morning to light the new fire. A popular riddle at the time relating to raking the fire went:

"As I sit on my hunkers,
I look through the golden ring,
I saw the dead bury the living,
I thought it a very curious thing."

Two other riddles in circulation then were,

"As I went through a guttery gap,

I met a boy with a red hat
A stick in his ass and a stone in his belly
Riddle me that and I'll give you a penny"

The answer was the red berry on a hawthorn bush.
The second riddle went,

"Upstairs and downstairs and windows made of glass
In the parlour chamber sits a bonny lass
With rings upon her fingers and bells upon her toes
A baby in her belly and off the lady goes".

The answer was a shotgun in a glass case in the hallway of a large house.

At dinner time a big fire would be blazing to boil the spuds. As soon as the spuds were boiled a scone was ready for baking in an oven which had a lid. Coals from the fire would be placed on the oven lid to ensure an even distribution of heat to bake the scone.

Before the coming of the egg incubator a man called McKeever had his own invention. He used a big pot lined with pieces of sheep's wool. He sat the pot beside the fire and put the hot ashes from the fire around the pot and this succeeded in generating the correct temperature for hatching hen eggs.

When turf was plentiful the fire stretched the full width of the hearth. As good hard black turf began to burn, one would notice the people move their chairs further and further down the kitchen floor. In most houses opposite the fireplace was the kitchen dresser. On the top three open shelves there were the shining and neatly placed delph. On the top shelf were the big willow patterned side plates, seldom used. On the middle shelf were the dinner plates. The bottom shelf was for a row of bowls wambled, that is upside down. At the bottom of the dresser sometimes having doors were the pots and pans. There were two big drawers in the centre. One held bread the other held the cutlery.

Most kitchens had a bed in the corner near the fire encircled by curtains. It was usually for the old people who were infirm. They could be warm in the kitchen and could see and hear all that was going on instead of being isolated in a bedroom. There were also a number of boles around the kitchen. Boles were a niche in the wall and sometimes they had shelves or were covered by a curtain. The boles were for storing various items of tobacco, groceries and other miscellaneous items.

The half door on a house was useful in keeping out the fowl which wandered around and fed in front of the house. It was not unusual to see a few hens perched on top of the half door. When a stranger would be coming to the house, the dog was first to make a move. Rising from the hearthside he would jump out over the half door, hens would fly and screech in all directions. The turkeys guldered, the ducks quacked and the geese screeched. A state of chaos would ensue before the visitor eventually entered the house.

The kitchen table was hinged to the wall with two front legs. It was hinged so that when the table was not in use it could be clipped up to the wall and leave more room in the kitchen for dancing. This table had a serious risk factor. When in use the two supporting legs could accidently get a knock and the legs would fold under the table sending delph and food crashing onto the flagstone floor. This sometimes happened when two dogs would get into a fight under the table. It once happened with my dog in Paddy Maguire's house.

When Mass was celebrated in a house in every townland in the parish during the seasons of Lent and Advent they were known as the house stations. Even the Protestant postman looked forward to the Station as he knew he would meet everyone in the townland under one roof and he would also get a cup of tea and time to enjoy any special fare prepared for the occasion. Preparations for the Stations included the whitewashing of the house inside and out. In later years bedrooms were papered. The house got a thorough cleaning and the street in front of the house would be scuffled free of grass and weeds. Sometimes the house got a new coat of thatch of rushes or straw.

After a Station Mass there would often be a lot of discussion amongst the gossips of how the house had been prepared for the Stations. There was a girl who lived next door to me who hadn't been to the local Station. She asked me about the station house and how it was done up. When I replied that I hadn't taken much notice. "You're a queer boy to go to a Station. When you go to the Stations the first thing you do is go to confession which is usually in the bedroom. You will see the wall in front of you when you are going in. Tell the priest something and look at the wall on your left, tell him something else and look at the wall on your right and on your way out you will see the other wall."

Like many other parts of Ireland at that time people spun their own yarn from sheep's wool and nearly every home hummed to the sound of the traditional spinning wheel. Weaving was also common with flax being a common commodity. Flax was pulled and left to soak in a large hole especially dug for the purpose and filled with water. These were known as lint dams. Later the flax was laid out to dry.

When the outside skin of the flax stalk was removed it revealed the linen fibre on the inside. Before the establishment of scutching mills the flax was laid on the roadway and a cart loaded with stones moved forward and backwards over the flax to break the outside skins. A scutching comb was then used to clean the remaining skin from the linen fibre. A scutching comb was like a hairbrush but with firm steel bristles.

One of the problems for home woven material was that it needed to be shrunk before garment making. This was achieved by treating the material in a solution from what was then called the "yarn pot". The yarn pot was a large ten gallon metal pot in which human urine was collected. This pot would be discreetly placed at dances in order that supplies were kept up. Added to the urine was pig manure and earth. The material was laid out on a level floor and this mixture was spread on top. This process had the effect of cleaning and pre-shrinking and thickening cloth prior to dying and manfacture into garments.

When I first relayed this story to locals I was not believed. However my story was vindicated when I received a tape from the Royal National Institute for the Blind talking book service, in which it gave an excerpt from a learned book on the English West Country woollen industry centred in Exeter. The author of this book confirmed that a similiar practice was operating in Exeter where it quotes that people were given the opportunity to earn a penny instead of spending one. The article in that book also made reference to the employees who used to walk all day through this mixture, pressing it into material, became known as walkers, from hence the family name Walker was derived.

Returning to the topic of linen the treated material was then stretched and held in tenterhooks in a wooden frame and laid out to bleach on a bleaching green. This was for the elements to do a natural process of bleaching. There was a bleaching green on the field on the right hand side of the lane into Carrick Street.

The youngsters of to-day may think it novel to have a picture of the latest pop stars on their tee shirts. In the nineteen twenties and thirties it was not unusual to spot the picture of 'The White Man' on a woman's shirt on a line of washing. Women had shirts made from flour bags under other garments. The 'White Man' was a picture forming the trademark on a popular brand of flour. Flour bags were also used for sheets and for making quilts.

In addition to making their own clothes, quilting was another use of cloth. To make a quilt a large wooden frame was required. Around this frame stood maybe up to ten women handsewing small pieces of material together in a colourful pattern. So when someone needed a quilt made, the young women were invited to the house and work would commence in the early afternoon. They would stop at about eight o'clock in the evening when the fellows would arrive and the night ended in a dance.

Shoes were also made at home and Carrick had its own shoemaker. The shoemaker would usually go from house to house measuring and tailor-making shoes for all in the family who required them. Shoes were made to cope with corns and bunions. The shoemaker would be seen to tack a piece of leather on to his wooden last to simulate the shape for a bunion.

There used to be government contracts which were called white sewing. These were nightdresses or locally called Chemise.

It was an opportunity for the womenfolk to make a small amount of money. A woman could make a dozen per week and was paid about three shillings. I remember Catherine Darcy and her sister hand sewing night after night under the limited light of a glass bottomed oil lamp. Barney her husband would make the tea. The women would say " here there's no need for you to be making the tay." Barney her husband would reply " I'm not making money so I'll make the tay." One of my favourite ceiliers to our house was Paddy Muldoon. Paddy used to take three pieces of lace trimmings and pleat three strands together. He would then cover them in black polish and use them as boot laces.

Another art of sewing was called sprigging or embroidery. Usually done on handkerchiefs by placing the cloth over a small hoop. A slightly larger hoop pushed down over the cloth causing it to become taut making it easier for the embroiderer to stitch.

One example of unusual craftsmanship happened one night in a house owned by a Robert Wier in a neighbouring townland of Glassmullagh. A number of fellows were in a house when a large delph serving plate big enough for the Christmas goose fell and split in two. With great ingenuity they managed to drill holes along the ends of the two broken pieces with an awl. They then sewed them together with wax end which was normally used for stitching shoes.

Nearly everyone had a sally garden. Sally rods were needed for basket making. If you wanted a basket made you had to supply the rods to the basket maker. Barney Darcy, my foster father, started me in this skill of basket making.

I remember him coming into the house one night with a bundle of rods. First he split a rod by placing it on his knee and putting a knife up through the centre. He then made two hoops out of the split rod and tied the ends with string and hung them up near the fireplace so as to season. When the hoops were seasoned one hoop was fitted inside the other to form the top ring of the basket. The ribs of the basket were rods bent with their ends springing against the inside of the basket rim. Finer rods were woven in and out around the ribs. A handle was attached to the rim on each side. The tunnac type of basket or half creel had many uses. They were used for carrying turf, collecting and washing potatoes, collecting eggs, holding seed potatoes for planting and many other uses. Other creels were the 'Kesh Creel', 'Burden Creel', 'Shoulder Creel', and a 'Manure Creel'.

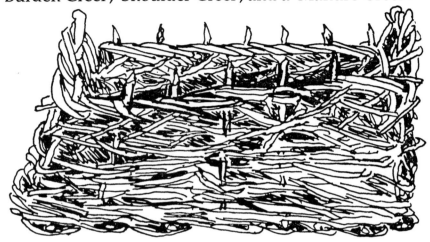

The Kesh Creel was used for carrying turf on a slipe. For a horse the creel measured six feet by four, for a donkey it measured three feet by two and a half feet. The depth of the 'Kesh Creel' was two and a half feet. The 'Burden Creel' was two feet by one foot at the mouth and tapered down two and a half feet in a cone-like shape. This creel had shoulder straps made from rushes or from cloth bags and was a very easy way to carry a load. Manys a youngster was carried in a burden creel. The 'Shoulder Creel' was a two foot square flat bottomed creel. It was used mainly to collect turf at a distance away from a cart. The flat bottom made it easier to carry on the shoulder. The 'Manure Creel' as its name suggests was for carrying manure from the dung heap or 'doughal' outside the cow byre to fertilise the fields. The Manure Creel measured two and a half feet by three feet and was used on a slipe.The 'Doughal' used to be a sign of wealth, the bigger the 'doughal' the greater the wealth, obviously a reflection on the size of a man's cowherd.

Dan Ferry showed me how to make súgán mats. Súgán mats were used for floors, mattresses, hen nests and covers for donkeys' backs. At that time there was at least one man in every townland who could do súgán work.

CHURNING MILK

Milk when taken from the cows was put into earthenware crocks. Crocks were large bowls about two feet in diameter. The milk was put into the crocks to allow it to settle and for the cream to come to the top. The cream was then skimmed off by tipping the crocks slightly to allow the cream to float off. The cream was then put into the churn. Large churns could hold up to twenty gallons. The dash was a long wooden shaft with a wooden plunger at the end. You had to pull the dash up to just under the surface of the milk and plunge down in an auger-like movement. Churning was a lonesome, monotonous operation. If you were fortunate enough to have a partner, each would have a "brash" (a go) for five minutes in rotation. When the butter came to the top of the churn it was put in a miskin. A miskin was an oblong shaped wooden box which held about ten pounds of butter and this was sold to the shops. The remaining butter was kept for the household and this was put into a print. The print was a wooden box with a handle which held about two pounds of butter. Most prints had a decoration of some kind carved inside the bottom of the print. When the butter was emptied out onto a plate the imprint was on top of the butter. Prints were made from sycamore as sycamore was easier for carving out designs. I remember John Connolly, the stonemason, cut a print of a thistle and seeing the raised print of the thistle on top of blocks of butter in the Connolly home.

CHAPTER SEVEN

Folklore

At that time when you "ceilied" in someone's house a member of the household "conveyed" you out to the end of their lane. Sometimes this was called being "conveyed past the gander" because ganders were plentiful and ganders were very cross. Ganders could be very dangerous as it was often said that a married man who didn't father a child probably got a nip from a gander.

On very dark nights some people would give their ceilier a lighted turf to carry. The wind would cause the turf to blaze up and throw a little light and provide some comfort in that the light would disperse any lurking ghosts or devils. The ceilier was often making his way home after a lenghty discussion on ghosts, fairies and black magic.

When darkness fell, people's imaginations rose. Logical explanations went out the window and superstitious beliefs came into peoples' minds. Catherine Darcy my foster mother once told me the story of how she as a young girl and all the local people were frightened one dark winter night. People could hear the massive roar of a bull coming from the mountain in the direction of Lough-A- Bradan. The Lough was about three miles away from Carrick. What had happened was that there had been a week of severe frost and Lough-A-Bradan had frozen over. The water level had dropped and the wind was blowing underneath the ice causing the deafening bull-like roar. High winds were greatly feared by the old people. On a very stormy night they would say "That night's as bad as the night of the big wind". This was a reference to the night of the big wind

115

which caused widespread damage throughout Ireland on the 3rd of September 1829.

Johnny Donnelly who lived in Carrick was afraid of ghosts and devils. He was walking home alone one night from a ceili in the townland of Carrickaness about five miles away. He could hear the rattle of chains coming behind him. That could only mean one thing, the devil himself must be following him. When Johnny stopped to listen the rattling of chains stopped. Eventually after a harrowing few hundred yards the chains came right up to him and said "ba-ba-a". It was a big billy goat with a chain around his neck who was out looking for some female company.

People used to describe how on sighting a ghost that they broke into a cold sweat and even one bald man claimed that the hair stood on his head. However most ghost stories and haunted houses were never rationally explained. One of the strangest ghost stories I heard was where a young woman died leaving five young children and a baby. Some months later in the middle of the night the children all jumped out of bed and congregated around the kitchen door. They jumped excitedly shouting " Mammy, Mammy Mammy". The baby was lifted from its cradle and was mysteriously carried around the room as if in someone's arms. The event was witnessed by the childrens' father and their grandmother although they could not see the woman.

There were a number of houses usually occupied by the bigger farmers which contained a locked room. These rooms were supposed to contain a lost soul or an evil spirit. I was in one house where I heard the eerie sound of a man walking around and around followed by the padding sound of a dog's feet coming from a locked upstairs room.

There was a house that had strange experiences where in

the middle of the night the dog would rise and fiercely fight some invisible stranger coming in the door. There was another house which I knew had a walled section in a room. There was a hole in the thatch which was visible on the outside. Everytime the roof was thatched attempts were made to cover up the hole but next morning the hole would reappear.

There was the story of a man who was walking late at night on the Glen Road at a spot which is known locally as "the gravel hill". Suddenly a man appeared in front of him on the road. Then the apparition disappeared and he heard something like a big bird flying up towards a house on the hillside. Forty years later a man on a bicycle coming past the same spot had a similiar experience.

There was a man called Mike Doran who was supposed to have read "The Black Book" which meant he was dealing in black magic. Mike shared a small farm in the townland of Cornavarra with his brother. Mike was a school teacher. He was once dismissed by the manager, the parish priest, because he put his own locks on the school door rather than have the inconvenience of having to travel every morning to the Parish Priest for the key. Mike was a popular teacher and had to be reinstated after parents withdrew their children from the school.

However Mike was a strange character. Someone met Mike at a cattle fair on a hot summer's day. He was wearing a long overcoat. He remarked to Mike that this was hardly suitable attire for such a hot day, Mike's explanation was that his coat kept out the cold in the winter so it should keep out the heat in the summer. He went on to explain that he was actually in the nude and the big coat allowed the air to circulate and keep him cool.

There was a story concerning Mike who was issued a pross or a summons by his landlord because he was behind with the rent. The pross server arrived to deliver his legal obligation. He found the door locked. There was a hole in the door where the latch should have been.

Mike was standing inside of the door and spoke in a stacatto childlike voice. "Put -in-your-finger like daddy does and lift the latch." The pross server duly obliged only to find that a razor instantly cut off the top of his finger. "Put-in-odder-finger now" continued Mike.

Another man who was dabbling in Black Magic apparently put his dark powers to good use. There was a hiring fair on the twelfth of May, a bright sunny morning. The landlord Patterson of Cooel had in his employment two young men and two young women. Their term extended to the autumn fair but the custom was that the hiring fair was like a public holiday, a break from the hard work and the promise of new or renewing aquaintances.

Patterson was a tough task master. He had six days cutting of turf on Dooish Mountain which were ready for footin'. So begrudgingly his hired hands trekked up the mountain to the turf banks. Now it was reckoned that it would take a man one day to foot one day's cutting of turf. The angry little group sat down complaining about the harshness of their employer.

After a time consternation broke out when someone spotted Patterson coming up the mountain. In the group was the man of the "Special Powers" who told them not to panic. He instructed them all to sit down again. Patterson disappeared from view when he came into a hollow in the mountain. The sorceror told them to keep watching down the mountain. He then placed two turf one on top of each other, placed four turf around the pair and placed one on top. "Now" he said " Four standing and one on the top". With that magical instruction the whole six days of cutting of turf was footed.

The group were sitting there when Patterson arrived. He knew something strange had happened but what could he do, the work was finished. So off down the mountain to the hiring fair went Patterson and his newly spirited employees. A few days later Patterson returned to the turf banks only to find that the six days cutting of turf all lying spread on the ground the same as the day they were cut. Also there were the two turf one on top of each other on which the sorceror had worked his black magic trick.

The sorceror also used his powers when meeting with a group of men sent to clear out the mud and slime which accumulated at the bottom of a lint dam. A lint dam was about fifteen yards long, three yards wide and six feet deep. Tons of mud and water would have to be removed with buckets. Three men were working on this job from morning to midday and although they worked hard they had made very little impression on the task.

The sorceror returned from his morning job of a delivery to the local creamery. Observing how little progress the men were making he suggested that they go in for their midday meal whilst he would use a bucket and would join them later. The three men were finishing their meal when our black magic man comes in and joins them. The three men returned to their task only to find the lint dam sparkling clean with piles of mud emptied out beside the dam. It is not known whether this was also an optical illusion in this instance or if the mud later returned to the dam.

The sorceror also used his powers to be released early

from his hiring contracts and still get his money. No one else could break a contract and get their money. The sorceror would scare the daylights out of a farmer and his wife and would have the table and chairs dancing through the house in the middle of the night. The farmer would gladly give the trickster his wages and let him go early.

Apart from the sorceror some people believed that their neighbours were practicing witchcraft. If a cow failed to give its normal supply of milk or the milk wouldn't turn to butter in the churn or if the cow was taken ill all these things were blamed on a neighbour using witchcraft against them. Danny Carr was reputed to be a man of special powers who could break evil spells. He visited the area and specialised in witchcraft that affected cattle.

Remembering that the average pay was a shilling per day Danny would charge a pound. That was not the full cost, because on Danny's instructions a farmer would be required to bury silver, four shillings and nine sixpence pieces at the stake of each cow to keep the evil spirits away. Danny was also known to go visiting former customers late at night with a spade.

Danny Carr played his part well. Usually a young person would be sent to fetch him. Danny would put on a show of dancing and gyration which would match some of today's pop stars. If you were walking with him at night he would suddenly stop in shock and proclaim "did you see that!" you would reply that you didn't see anything "well it's just as well that you didn't" Danny would respond.

Danny Carr was able to take advantage of people's superstitious beliefs. People believed that a woman could turn herself into a hare and suck the milk from her neighbour's cow. Some people were given to a "bad eye" and caused problems for your cows, if the bad eye were cast upon them. No one ever entered a cow byre without saying good luck to your cattle and if you didn't it was regarded that you meant bad luck to them.

A case in point is where a man had little grass for his cow so he took the cow to graze along the roadside or what was commonly called "the long acre". However on one occasion a traveller on the road was passing, and in admiration of the cow said to the farmer "that's a lovely wee cow, I wish she was mine". The owner immediately brought the cow home and closed her in the byre for three days.

Danny Carr's secret of success was that he knew that boiling water killed the evil of bacteria. Most problems were resolved when Danny's prescription to scrub and scald all utensils connected with milking and churning. However Danny was found out in the end. This happened when an old man called on Danny's services because his cow's milk would not produce butter.

Before his arrival Danny gave the instructions to have ready a bottle of whiskey, a large barrel full of spring water, seven milk cans and two candles. Danny arrived late at night to perform his excorcism of the evil one who was interfering with the cow's milk. Danny cautioned the old man that it was going to be a long difficult night to rid him of this evil one. So Danny suggested a glass of whiskey to help calm the nerves. The old man rarely ever touched alcohol and Danny insisted on him taking several glasses and the old man became quite intoxicated. "Now" said Danny "the hour has arrived". "You must watch me and do exactly everything as I do" instructed Danny.

He gave the old man one of the lighted candles and told him that they would walk slowly towards the barrel of spring water. Danny gave the old man a handkerchief but by the poor light of the candle he did not notice that Danny had dipped it in red paint. Danny took one step and wiped his brow with the handkerchief, the old man obediently followed. Another slow step and Danny wiped the handkerchief across his mouth. So step by step and wiping the handkerchief across their faces with the candles held in their hands the two men arrived at the barrel of water. "Now look into the barrel of water and you will see the boyo who is spoiling your milk" advised Danny.

The old man who had a white beard peered into the water and saw his reflection by candlelight. The sight of his white beard and his face covered with several red streaks caused the old man to shout "Good God isn't he the bad looking brute". Danny gave the usual instructions to boil all utensils. However the evil drink got to Danny that night and neighbours found Danny and the old man next morning fast asleep with his painted face.

In 1920 there was a local woman who believed that my foster mother Catherine Darcy could turn herself into a hare and was sucking the milk from her cows. So firmly did she believe this that she used to tie red rags on the cows tails to dispell the approaches of the bewitched hare. There was also a belief that the hare could only be killed by a silver bullet. However, Catherine Darcy did not take too kindly to the suggestion that she was haring around the countryside taking the milk from the neighbours cattle. Catherine took a case against the woman and it was heard by a Sínn Féin court as the British court was not recognised by both parties in dispute. The court directed the woman to stop making the allegation and there was never a word spoken about witchcraft in Carrick since then.

122

The Sínn Féin court reminds me of a story of when the court was in session in a hall near Drumquin. A man who ran into the hall to alert the court that British soldiers were coming, was heard to shout " Lie down on your belly your honour, the soldiers are coming"!

The first day of May was surrounded by superstitious beliefs. The spring well would be surrounded by the yellow May flowers by the first person to draw water from the well. There was also the practice that the first person to draw water on the first May morning would put a 'jap' (splash) of water on the stone at the front of the well to indicate that they had been to the well first and had drawn 'good luck'.

CURES

Some people seemed to have special powers to cure ailments but there was also the herbal type cures. Nettles were boiled for measles, the boiled root of rhubarb was used as a cure for constipation. Rheumatism was treated with a teaspoonful of honey, treacle and cider vinegar in warm water taken night and morning. A piece of an eel skin was worn on a sprained wrist or ankle. A sprain was usually referred to as a tállagh.

The Maguire family in Carrick had the cure for ringworm. This usually took the form of using an ink pen to mark the boundries of the affected area. Ringworm was more common then, probably because people had greater contact with cattle.

A cure for heart fever, a slowing down of the heart beat involved using oatmeal. The cure worker would fill a glass with oatmeal and then walk around the believing sufferer until the oats settled and sank in a glass. The sufferer was then instructed to take the oatmeal home and make porridge and eat it. There was a Mrs. Bradley from Drumquin who went for this cure. She was sceptical of its powers and related to me how she came home and in her words made stir-a-bout (porridge) from the oatmeal and gave it to the hens.

A cure for mumps was bestowed onto the first born of a couple who bore the same surnames before they were married. The cure worker would put a donkey's winkers or halter on the head of the sick person and led them three times around a spring well.

There was a woman by the name of McPhilomey who had a cure for a moate in the eye. This was a fairly common complaint at that time as people were more likely to be involved in dusty work conditions like flailing corn. The moate victim did not need to visit the cure worker. You could send someone else to her house. Mrs. McPhilomey would take out a full glass of water and then disappear for a while to her bedroom. She would return a short time later with the moate floating on top of the water. Even though the victim maybe ten miles away they would be relieved of their moate.

There was a belief that a mother's milk was a cure for sore eyes. There was a story of a little lad of nine years who had this complaint. His mother sent the little fellow with a note to a neighbouring woman. The neighbouring woman read the note and told the little lad to sit down on a stool. This fine buxom woman stood in front of the young lad, lifted her blouse and hit him with a splash of milk in the eye and almost knocked him off the stool. Then she told him to run off home and that his eyes would get better.

There was a man from the neighbouring County of

Fermanagh who married a local girl. He was a very remarkably neatly dressed wee man. If he was going to work for a farmer he would put on his best suit, collar and tie and his shoes would be shining as he went off to work. He would then change into his working clothes and at the end of the day change back into his suit. His wife was once heard to remark that her wee Paddy was so neat and clean that he never dirtied his trousers.

His wife developed a sore knee and was advised to go to a Tommy Russell who lived near Ederny for a cure. So off went Paddy and his wife. Now at that time the women wore great long skirts down to their ankles. In order for Tommy to perform his cure the knee had to be rubbed.

So he reached down and lifted the great skirt and with that the wee man shouted " don't do that". He immediately took his wife home without the cure.

There was a man called McMenamin who had a cure for warts. A neighbouring man had a son covered in warts. So he met with McMenamin outside the chapel gate after Sunday Mass, which was the usual meeting place for such contacts. He told McMenamin about his son. McMenamin called the boy over to him and then gave him a shove. The next morning the boy was completely cured of the warts.

There were also two wart wells near Carrick. One was located in the Glen between Donnelly's Croft and O'Kanes land on the east side of Carrick. The well was a round hole about 3" in diameter and 3" deep on a large flat stone at the edge of the stream which gushed down the glen. During heavy rainfall the rushing water would splash out and fill up this little miracle well. The other well for curing warts was similar and was located at the edge of the stream which flows under Corlishog bridge.

Barney Darcy my foster father had the cure for a burn. The cure was for him to lick the back of a 'Thomologue' or 'Mankeeper' a member of the lizard family found in marshy ground. Barney had then to lick the victim's burn.

Although some animals were important for cures there were others that had the opposite effect. One such animal was the weasel or as we called it the 'whithred'. The whithred's spittle was poisonous and one would avoid interfering with it in anyway. There was a local man who was mowing one day and he accidentally disturbed a whithreds nest. Later in the day he saw a whithred spitting into his small can of drinking water.

CHAPTER EIGHT

Hard work

The hardest and most dispiriting work done was that demanded from landlords. The last of the landlords I remembered lived at Liskey near Drumquin village. He was landlord for most of the land in Carrick and in the Glen areas. There are various stories about landlords but a local example was of a landlord called Stack.

He expected you to work for him as a means of paying his rent. He evicted a sick old man who had the money to pay the rent but the old man refused to toil for him.

One man who worked for Stack managed to save up seven pounds. He decided to buy a cow. He left late in the evening after a hard day's work for Stack and walked across the mountains to a fair in Donegal Town. There he purchased a cow. He had to return by the road with the cow and arrived home two mornings later. All he had eaten in approximately thirty six hours was the heart of a cabbage he took from a garden. He had given the outer leaves to the cow. When he got home his son was setting out to go to work on the landlord's farm five miles away. He asked his son to wait a few minutes until he got some porridge and then he came with him for the day's work.

Landlord Stack had a steward named Rogers. Rogers would come up the Glen Road to Carrick in a pony and trap blowing a whistle. This was the signal for every tenant farmer to drop his own work and follow him. You had to go immediately even if you were saving your own hay. There were occasions when men were in their hay fields and were summoned by the whistle to go off for two day's work. This involved moving stones from one heap to a heap in another field and then returning them to the original field.

The landlord's steward would push men into drains if they tried to work from a dry spot in making drains. Men were used to plough just like horses. There were four men pulling and one holding the plough to cut the scores. Landlords died out around the 1920's.

The twelfth of May was the traditional date for the hiring fair. Young men and women made themselves available to be hired by the big farmers. A six month contract for hard labour and you only received pay at the end of the six months provided you served the full term. There was no such thing as severence pay. If you left your employment early you lost your six months wages. There were many examples where employers did their best to get you to leave early so as to avoid paying the wages.

LIMESTONE

In the townland of Carrick I remember two small limestone kilns. Each which would burn about one ton of limestone. Strangely one seemed to be built with clay. There was one located near Dungormley Fort and the other at Hollands Rock about a mile apart. When the Tyrone and Fermanagh Hospital was being built in Omagh these kilns supplied lime for the building mortar. The lime in the mortar provided extremely good bonding qualities.

The limestone was burnt with turf. Often workers would have to stay up at night with the burning kiln as turf burned very fast. About a twelve inch layer of turf would burn a broken layer of limestone rocks three inches deep.

This process was called eekin. These broken stones would have been "knapped" that is broken into about one and a half inch in diameter with a small hammer known as a knapping hammer. Coal was not used locally in burning limestone until after the Second World War in the mid 1940's.

Burnt limestone was used to scatter on ground prepared in ridges for the setting of potatoes. As access to much of the land was soggy and boggy the lime was carried in creels by the men and sometimes by the women. Good limestone was that which had lumps which were partially burnt, known as the hearts. Limestone which was thoroughly burnt was not considered good. Burnt limestone was also spread on grassland at approximately one ton per acre.

In 1941 a large scale production of burnt limestone commenced. A major employer in the area was James Moffatt who opened a quarry in Dunaree beside the ancient fort. Moffatt was a very fair employer. I went to work for him as a kiln man.

The first stage in quarrying limestone was to raise boulders in the quarry. Gelignite was used. A hole had to be made into the rock with hand-held steel drills with another man striking the drill with a sledge hammer. It usually took the two men an hour to drill twelve inches into the rock. The gelignite came in candle-like sticks and were pushed down into the drilled holes. A detonator cap and fuse wire were then connected to the gelignite.

One man whose job it was to detonate the explosive used to remark dryly when warning his work mates, " look out boys I'm just going up here to let off a wee poff". A short time later the blast would send a shower of rocks and boulders tumbling down the quarry face.

This limestone quarry was part of a limestone seam that runs from Belfast to Bundoran in County Donegal. It was interesting to note the differences in the seams of limestone which occured at Dunaree and that in Carrick four miles away. In Dunaree the layer formations were horizontal whilst in Carrick the formations were vertical. Occasionally we came across fish fossils in the stones.

The large boulders had to be broken into smaller pieces using a fourteen pounds sledge hammer. These stones were then transported by lorry to a small breaker near the lime kiln. There the mechanically driven breaker would break the stones even smaller before being transported by wheelbarrow to the lime kiln.

Breaking stones was an art in its own right. When you were confronted with a large boulder you first had to check how the layers of limestone were formed. Using steel punches about eighteen inches long and half an inch in diameter the human stone breaker using a four pound hammer would punch a line of small holes along a seam in the layers about three inches apart. Then a larger steel punch was used and using the fourteen pound sledge hammer the punches were given a fairly stong blow. The force of the blow had to be carefully measured and not a crashing blow. Very soon the large boulders would split in two.

Layers of stone in the quarry were hard and soft. The soft layers were at the top and bottom of the quarry with the hard layers in the middle. At the kiln one had to recognise the differences. In loading the kiln, stones were measured by the barrow full. A barrow-full was about two hundred weight.

Firstly twelve barrow-fulls of hard stones were put in

using steel grapes and levelled. Then two barrow-fulls of coal formed the next layer. This was followed by fifteen barrow-fulls of the softer stones. This alternating process of a layer of hard stones, coal and soft stones continued until the kiln was full. The fire was lighted at the bottom of the kiln and burned its way up through the various layers. The kiln produced ten tons of burnt limestone per day. The burnt limestone or lime, as it was called was shovelled into one hundred weight bags and stacked in five ton lots. A quarry man's pay in 1941 was three pounds per week. This increased to seven pounds per week after the end of World War Two in 1945.

FLAX

In 1937 and 1938 there was a government grant for growing flax. Fields of the blue blossomed plant could be seen around the countryside. There was a small industry in digging lint dams. These were holes in the ground filled with water in which the harvested flax was steeped. This was to soften and loosen the outer skin of the flax stalk which would later be removed. Removal would reveal the hard central fibre which was used in making linen.

The flax when harvested was bundled in sheathes about the thickness of a telegraph pole and tied with a strap made of rushes. When the time came to remove the flax from the lint dams the men had to wade in waist deep in slimey water. They had to lift the sheaves out onto the broo or the sides of the dam. These men were often given whiskey to counter the chill from the cold water of the dam. The wet sheaves had to be opened and the rush band had to be left aside to be used later in the harvesting process.

The stocks of flax were laid out neatly in rows in the field where the flax once stood. When the flax dried it was put back into sheathes and tied again with the original rush bands. The sheathes were then built into a stack and later brought to a scutching mill.

In the mill the outer skin of the stocks were removed. When a group of neighbours got together to harvest flax or any other crop this was called a banwal or meitheal. Generally after a banwal a dance would be held, a sort of celebration of an accomplishment.

The arrival in the farm yard of the touring corn threshing mill was another opportunity for community endeavour. The thresher would be pulled by a tractor into the haggard beside the corn stacks. There would be a great lot of fussing about as the thresher was levelled before operations began.

There would be two men up on the thresher, one cutting straps of the sheaves of corn the other feeding the corn into the machine. One or two men on the corn stack, a man or two clearing away the headless straw from the bottom of the thresher. There would be a man hooking on the bags into which the thresher poured the golden grain whilst another sewed, sealed and stacked the big bags of grain. The young people would be chasing the hoards of rats that would be disturbed from the corn stacks. The visit of the thresher was viewed more as an amusement rather than work.

MOWING

A scythe had to be correctly balanced and properly set. A scythe is a more complicated instrument than it first appears. There is the blade, then there is the sned, that is the long wooden shaft onto which two short handles are attached. First you got your blade and brought it to the local blacksmith. The blacksmith adjusted the tang an L shaped piece of metal at the handle end of the blade. The higher the tang the lower the blade was for cutting. It also enabled the mower to stand straighter.

The blade was fixed by the tang through a metal ring on the sned and wedged with an iron and maybe a wooden wedge. You then put the bottom of the sned to where the blade was attached under your armpit and reached up the shaft and a handle would be positioned at the point of your fingers.

Next you put your elbow to this handle and the second

handle was fixed where your fingers now touched further up the shaft or sned. This emphasises how a scythe had to be set to suit the build of the individual mower.

A test for the sharpness of the blade was that it could "cap a lap". The mower should be able to cleanly cut the top off a lap of hay without disturbing the position of the lap. The mower should then be able to mow hay or corn with little effort just using the weight of the scythe swinging to make the cut. Another test for sharpness was to check if the blade could cut the hairs off your arm.

Sharpening the blade was another skill. In using the sharpening stone you placed the stone near the edge of the blade and then pulled, placing greater weight initially and then easing off as the stone left the blade. A good mower could mow three roods of hay in a day.

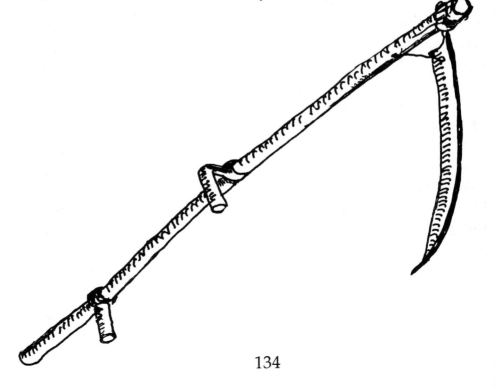

USING A SPADE

Sousing was a job preparing the ridges for the planting of potatoes. This involved pegging a line of cord in a straight line. Then using the spade sideways a track was ripped in the earth up along the line. Then the line was moved to form a gap of about six inches and the process was repeated.

Then you dug out the clay between the two tracks and threw it left or right onto the centre of what now would become a ridge for planting. Ridges were about four and a half feet wide ending up about three feet wide when the final process of planting was completed. This stage was followed by spreading manure on the ridge and then dropping three seed potatoes three inches apart across and lengthwise on the ridge about fifteen inches apart.

The seed was then covered up digging a sod along the edge of the soused track. Later when the potato plants emerged just above the surface of the ground the loose clay in the trenches between the ridges was shovelled up forming small mounds around each of the new plants.

At thirteen years of age I was able to open and set an acre of potatoes, about a month's work.

Spade work also involved in digging drains. A form of drain used in mossy ground was to dig a shallow trench. Then, using a turf spade, a deep narrow cut was made at the bottom of the trench. This was then covered over with dried out parings from turf banks. Large stones were used as coverings if they were accessible.

During one winter Tom Connolly of Carrick and his brother found themselves with no work. So they decided to pass the time using foot spades. They dug up seven acres and left it ready for the planting of corn in the Spring.

Tom Connolly told me about one time when his father found himself with the rent due and had no money. So one day after building a stack of corn he continued through the night and threshed with a flail. Corn was flailed on a barn door lying in the middle of a large cloth which was called a winning cloth. That night Tom Connolly's father threshed enough corn to fill a two hundredweight sack. This he took the next day to Drumquin and sold it to get the money to pay the rent.

HAYMAKING

After mowing and being fortunate enough to have a few good dry days, hay had to be turned over using a wooden rake. If you were really lucky and the weather continued, the hay would be shaken using a pitchfork which would then leave the hay ready for building into ricks or as locally we called them rucks.

However most years, rain would intervene in the harvesting of the hay. Damp weather would initiate a hated process called lapping. This involved shaking the hay by hand into loose bundles folding them over your arm and setting the bundle of hay lightly on the ground. The lap had to be loose and open in order for the hay to dry. This was a slow monotonous tedious job.

For children in particular it was the most hated process in haymaking. Apart from the extra hours one had to spend in the hay field one had to cope with the thistles and the odd stalk of hay going up your nose, a most unpleasant tingling sensation, causing your eyes to water. Children fast developed backache amongst the list of complaints in which to get excused from lapping hay.

Building the rucks of hay was fun. The dried hay was gathered in and raked into a circle. Children would run with armfuls and laps of hay and roll in the mound of hay being prepared for building. A ruck was built by laying a base with a pitchfork. A builder then stood in the middle and spread the forkfuls of hay evenly around the ruck.

One always had to make sure that the very dry hay went into the heart of the ruck. This was put under the feet of the builder. As the ruck rose in height it became more unsteady and if you were the builder you always had to be on the lookout in case you got a dab of the pitchfork in your legs.

The rucks of hay had to be secured using hay ropes. The ropes were made by feeding strands of hay onto a twister. A twister was made from bull wire bent into a shape to look like the starting handle of an old motor car. Some pieces of hollowed out boortree were used as handles to make the twisting operation easier on your hands.

As rope making involved two operators, usually the younger folk, there were inevitable rows. The twister would be going too fast or the feeder feeding too slow and the rope would break.

MODEL FARMERS

William MacVeigh was the eldest of the family of fourteen. All the family emigrated except William. He was skilled in making baskets, carpentery and making shoes. MacVeigh was a neat worker.

There was a family called Walker who lived near William. The Walker man died relatively young leaving two sons. William taught the two sons all the arts of farming and turf cutting with the result as grown men the young Walkers were very neat and exact farmers.

I used to cut turf for them. This was a privilege as one had to be a master craftsman to be employed by the Walkers. The turf had to be cut in such a way that the face of the turf bank was left smooth and shining. There were not to be any evidence of nicks from the turf spade. Even the top sods had to be cut in neat squares and laid evenly in the bog hole like a regular patterned carpet.

Their turf barrows, although over forty years old, looked almost new. They would not allow any litter to be left behind after eating on the mountain and their house and farmyard was a model of neatness.

In the townland of Cooel was a family called Marshall who also exemplified neatness in their farming methods. The Marshall's father wore his wedding suit and shoes every Sunday up until he died aged seventy or over. The Marshalls always paved their land drains with stones even the mountain drains. They had an orchard and were very generous with apples to children. I remember there were three men living in the house and when I entered they would all rise together to greet me.

In the same townland there was another family who was

a model of neatness and economy called "the groom" McCanny's. The Grooms like the Marshalls rarely ceilied and would spend their spare time threshing corn in the barn or repairing and tidying up the farmyard. On one rare occasion the eldest of the three brothers, Barney, led his brothers by hurricane lamp to the Marshall's home.

The purpose of this rare excursion was to exchange methods of economising. After initial greetings the economic talks began. Davey the eldest of the Marshalls got up and blew out the lamp. Lesson number one, save the oil. Then by the light of the fire he showed the Grooms how to save wear on their trousers. He lowered his trousers to the knees when sitting down at the fire. The Marshalls also explained how they would take the sheet from their beds in the morning, catch it at each of the four corners and dust off the bran. The bran would have accumulated on their bodies during the flailing of corn. This was then dusted into a bucket and fed to the hens.

Davey Marshall had a little small bodied horse. It was twenty two years old. The horse had a bad stomach and could not eat grass as it made it sick. Davey trained the horse not to eat grass by shouting at it "drop that" everytime it attempted to graze. Davey's animal training came to his own rescue when he was an old man living on his own. He had fallen and broken his leg. By good fortune he had a pot of boiled potatoes sitting in the corner of the kitchen. He got the dog to carry the potatoes one at a time to keep himself fed until help arrived at the house three days later.

TURF CUTTING

Turf cutting was completed with neighbouring men giving each other " a day in the bog" . Normally a year's supply of turf was the work of three men for three days cutting. One man cut, one filled or lifted the cut sods whilst another shovelled the cut sods or wheeled them out in a barrow and spread them out to dry on the turf banks. On a shallow bank one turf deep it was cut twelve turf wide or approximately four feet in width. Where the turf moss ran deeper to three turf or more the bank was cut nine turf wide. Work had to be completed in a rhythm like fashion.

Turf had to be laid lengthwise onto the shovel. The shovel had to arrive in time to collect from the lifter so as not to break his momentum. Wheelbarrows had to be exchanged without causing a break in the sequence of work. The top layer or floor of turf was wheeled out and emptied in rows leaving a gap of about nine feet where the next floor was shovelled out in neat rows with turf lying parallel to the turf bank.

A good days cutting of turf was twelve turf wide, fifty yards long and three turf deep, about twelve cart loads. In the 1930's to hire a man for a day's work in the bog was three shillings the same as for mowing. General labouring was two shillings or richer farmers paid half a crown per day. I cut my turf on Carrick Mountain. We would set off early morning with two turf barrows, turf spade, two ordinary spades for paring the sods off the turf banks and a shovel. As we would spend a full day on the mountain we took with us a basket of homemade bread, a bottle of milk and a can of spring water for making tea.

When the turf dried a hard crust formed. The turf would

now be turned over or spread to increase the drying process. When a crust had formed on all four sides of the turf it could now be footed, the final stage in the drying process. Footin' consisted of laying two turf one on top of each other and propping a number of other turf around these. When it came to bringing the turf home a horse and slipe would be used as the mountain was too soft for carts.

A slipe was like a wide ladder which had two long shafts which went on each side of the horse with the other end sliding along the ground. The two shafts were held together behind the horse by four planks across. Metal pins were driven into each shaft about eighteen inches from where the shaft touched the ground. The purpose of the pins were to help fix creels or large baskets of turf onto the slipe. A horse was able to take six loads from Carrick Mountain in a day.

Tom Connolly of Carrick had seven brothers and two sisters and lived with his widowed mother. A neighbouring man called Paddy Ferry and Mickey McCanny were giving their shared stint in the bog. So one sunny morning Tom,

Paddy and Mickey set off for the mountain with all their acutrements. There was a bonus in that Tom's sisters would trudge their way up the mountain in the middle of the day with a dinner of spuds and mutton stew. The stew was carried in gallon tin cans wrapped in old pieces of blankets to keep the dinner warm.

When the three turf cutters had completed the long climb of a mile they were hot and worst of all they were thirsty. Water was not enough to quench the thirst and being a hot day they expected to have even greater dreuth in their mouths when the work got underway. Mickey McCanny was reckoned to be the fastest traveller. He was dispatched to make a two mile trek across the other side of the mountain and procure stronger stuff for a man's thirst in a pub in the village of Lack in County Fermanagh.

Meanwhile Tom and Paddy pared the sods off the turf bank. Mickey returned sometime later with a bag of bottles. Full of good intentions they tanked up in preparation for a day's cutting. Tom's sisters arrived with the dinner and observed that there was no turf cut. The three fellows were too busily engaged in an advanced stage of the long jump competition.

The girls tried to intervene but had to deposit the dinner and return home. The three cutters jumped all day and came home late in the evening with the dinner untouched. Tom's mother brought her son into the house and chased his two accomplices home.

This story of thirst getting in the way of cutting turf has been repeated a good few times in the locality and even as recent as the 1980's. This involved three characters who were under the influence before setting out. They got one barrow-full of turf cut. The barrow-man set off rather wobbly to deposit his load, normally about twenty yards away. However, he was so well fuelled that he just kept going across the heather clumps and marshes and disappeared from view.

The turf cutter watching this with bewilderment and with alcoholic imbalance fell on top of his assistant and both ended up soaked, this time with real mountain dew.

CHAPTER NINE

The new era

The ending of the Second World War in 1945 and later the implementation of a Social Welfare System under the newly elected Labour government in Britain brought radical changes. Children went to secondary schools and University. The nature of employment changed dramatically. The young people were now getting jobs as nurses, in trades and other professions. Before 1948 three shillings and sixpence was the employer's half of a social welfare weekly stamp. This entitled you to 17/6d per week for unemployment or sickness benefit. However, I joined the Irish National Foresters and for one shilling per week I got a free doctor, free hospital and ten shillings per week for sickness benefit. If you got married you got five pounds and if you had a funeral in the family you got fifteen pounds.

In the period 1920 until 1945 I was fortunate to witness many firsts in the locality.

The arrival of the first tractor and the first car were historical events in their own right. The first tractor arrived in the area around 1939. A man called Nethery had a big heavy Fordson tractor which bore the notice "first in the field and still leading". The first car that came up the Glen Road was spotted by Mickey "Vickey" McCanny, Paddy Ferry and Tom Connolly.

They were cutting turf on Carrick Mountain a mile from the Glen Road. They heard the noise of the car coming about two miles away. They dropped their spades and shovels and ran to see the car. The car was owned by a veterinary surgeon.

Later the three men described the great event of this space invader parked with it's engine running. They related their story to a hushed fireside audience later that night of seeing a car jumping up and down with the occasional pop.

The occasion enabled me to collect a few items of transport history during those discussions on the development of transport. I discovered that the Glen Road was made in 1847. Prior to that there was just a track for the pack horses. The pay was ten pence a day. The contractor's name was O'Brien and one hundred men were employed on the job.

Catherine Darcy my foster mother related how she accompanied funerals to Langfield Church. She remembered coffins being carried over four miles by handspokes. Four people carried the coffin, two each side with the coffin resting on two round poles. People carried the coffin in relays in distances of one hundred yards. The relief crew were able to make the change over without a break in stride.

The local historians made categoric statements that the first cart in the area with spoke wheels was around 1900. Up until then carts had solid wood or log wheels. There were stories of how the building stones of St. Patrick's Church in Langfield were drawn to the site on log wheel carts. So also were the stone pillars of Omagh Courthouse which were quarried at Kirlish near Drumquin.

At that time horse transport was very much in vogue. Paddy Ferry had a trap, as did Hugh Maguire, Patrick Byrne, William McVeigh and Eugene McLoughlin. Tom "Mor" McCanny, Pat Gallogly, Paddy Maguire and the Carrolls had jaunting cars. A man named Eoin Gilleece had a little trap and a jennet.

The other mode of transport was of course the bicycle. Raleigh bikes were the best quality but were the most expensive at five pounds. That was the equivalent of six month's pay. Tom Connolly and Paddy Ferry were the first in Carrick to purchase bicycles. Bicycles had become very plentiful around 1932.

In 1932 the Eucharistic Congress was held in Dublin. In recognition of this event Mass was celebrated at the Penal Mass Rock in Corridinna in the parish of Drumragh near Omagh. It was attended by about four thousand people. There were hundreds and hundreds of bicycles parked along the roadside leading to the Mass Rock. I remember great attention being paid to the only motor cycle present. I remember the owner was a woman who wore brown leather knee length boots laced in a criss-cross fashion. There were horses and traps but no motor cars.

In the 1920's the grocery delivery vans were all horsedrawn. There was a grocery van owned by Campbells of Dromore, County Tyrone. Their van used to come to Corlishog Bridge and turn there. A lot of people met the grocery van there and exchanged groceries for eggs and homemade butter. The driver's name was Willie Lowe. He used to arrive on Fridays at about four o' clock in the afternoon when the children were coming home from school. I remember we used to run after the horse and van down the road. We liked Willie Lowe. He was tall, dark skinned, long faced, quiet, aloof man. We used to hop onto a space in the back of the van.

The year was 1920 and the struggle for Irish Independence had touched our part of Ireland. The Irish Republican Army had placed a boycott on the sale of Gallagher's tobacco. However, Campbell hadn't heeded the warning. We were coming from school one Friday and as usual expecting to see Willie Lowe and Campbell's van parked at Corlishog Bridge.

First we met two men with guns by their sides. They didn't take any notice of us. We stopped to look at the guns but they told us to move on. Further down the road at what used to be an old school house, Campbell's van was ablaze. The mare had been freed and bolted. I can remember the fierce heat of the blazing wooden boxes as we passed by. By strange coincidence, sixty years later Willie Lowe Junior visits me driving a library van, delivering tapes and books for the eldery and the disabled.

The first gramophone which came to the locality was purchased by "Red" Frank McCanny. That was in 1926 when I was thirteen years old. I remember going to "Red" Frank's house to see the gramophone for the first time. I was with my pal who was aged twelve, Alphonsus O'Kane, who later became a priest. Frank's wife was out and Frank made us tea. I can still remember Frank cutting us big thick slices of homemade cake. We sat all day listening to the great tenor John McCormack and Scots singer Harry Lauder coming out of the big horn of the gramophone.

The radio came next and newspapers became more available. The first wireless to come to the area was in 1937 which was purchased by Meehan, the stone cutter. It had no aerial and you wouldn't have heard it behind a wet newspaper.

One of the advantages in living in a remote rural area was that one could avoid paying the licence for their wireless which most people took advantage of. The strategy was that if you purchased a wireless you should never licence it because you were now on record and the authorities would keep checking up on you to ensure your annual payment. Post office officials would periodically conduct a campaign to check on unlicenced wireless listeners. As soon as a licence inspector checked the first house on the Glen Road a hot line went into operation.

This usually involved bread delivery men, cyclists, children and anything that moved up the Glen road. Wireless's would be put in a sack and hidden in ditches until the alert was over. I remember on one occasion in 1956 the alert had been raised. I was not at home but my wife realised that our licence was overdue. Duly she put the wireless in the sack and dispatched it to the security of a large clump of nettles. My wife had another dilemma. She hated telling lies. A few days before she had the misfortune to have her face badly burned in an accident involving a tilly lamp. To relieve the pain of the burn she used pink coloured calamine lotion. The calamine lotion turned out to be a saviour. The licence inspector asked her "Do you have a radio in the house"? Her honest answer was "No" because it was hidden in the clump of nettles. My wife admitted later that the calamine lotion had covered her blushes.

The improvements in transport and communications brought a short lived hope that more people could stay at home. The reverse happened. Better communications confirmed to the youth that there was greener grass on other sides of the world. Who would blame them. There was no work. Rural communities did not seem to matter to government policy makers. The piped water service and mainline electricity was not brought to Carrick nor the Glen until 1970. As a result young families fled the area to bigger towns whilst the older couples could only avail of modern amenities in a County Council Housing Estate in Drumquin. For the older people like myself who moved out it was a feeling of having deserted your roots. Forestation was part of the deal. Some were enticed to sell off their mountain

148

pastures to the Forestry Service. Our land was considered to be only fit for the planting of trees.

The landscape is becoming uniform. Hundreds of acres are now in plantation. The townlands of Meenaheeri and most of Carrowadowa and the lower slopes of Tappaghan Mountain near Cooel is blotted with various undistinguishable species of evergreen trees. Carrick has escaped so far but it is being surrounded on all sides by the invading forest.

There was a local man, the late Louis McLaughlin, who on first hearing of forestery plantation propositions jokingly predicted the consequences. Said Louis " in a short time there will be no one left in this Glen. There will be a forestry gate at Dooish Crossroads and another at Annaghlough Crossroads. There will be nothing only trees and a rough track for the forestry workers."

Lough-A-Bradan is now surrounded by forestry plantation. The ancient Cairn and passage grave nearby remain in a small clearing. In the 1930's a neighbour of mine Barney McGrath was emigrating to Scotland. As a parting gift he gave me hard black pear shaped stone. Barney used to use it for sharpening his razor. I found it too hard for the razor but fortunately I kept the stone. In recent years my son-in-law from County Mayo spotted the stone. He recognised it as an ancient stone axe head dated approximately 3000 to 5000 B.C. I donated the axe head to the National Museum in Dublin. It was then that I made the connection with the ancient passage grave. Barney McGrath used to live close to it. I presume he found it around there and like me did not recognise its significance.

What a shame it will be if the next generation does not recognise the significance of this historic and beautiful natural countryside. Is it to be lost in the undergrowth of a forest? I am glad that my last sight of Carrick is one that I dearly cherish. I only hope that this book in some way prevents the loss of the true landscape of Carrick. I have felt a responsibility to pass on to you the history and folklore of Carrick and I hope you will treasure my contribution as much as the people of Carrick who passed it on to me.

I will conclude with the following verse to summarise my love for Carrick.

CARRICK

It stands there in the valley, beneath the mountain crest
Well known to all is Carrick, the place I love the best
Surrounded by its high green hills, the hazel and the whin
Adjacent to the leading road, from Ederny to Drumquin.

Oh Carrick is rich in folklore and beauty unsurpassed
With its many forts and fairy glens and memories of the past
It was here O'Neill a sword did wield when
Maguire he pressed him hard
When his vanguard fought at Garrison, a mile from Carrickard.

How pleasant to see the sun come up o'er
Tappaghan's heathery crest
And shine gently down on Carrick 'till it sets far in the west
From the mountain top you can see afar Lough Erne lying low

And the whitewashed walls of Carrick so peaceful there below.

Duncannon Fort stands on the green and Holland's rock so high
You can gaze right down on Haughey's town
with the river running by
And the mountain face where a hardy race made
the landscape rich and green
And the low green hills, the drumlins, are plainly to be seen.
Dungormley Fort on the hillside nearby the Fairy Glen
Where we were told that in days of old dwelt little fairy men
And often in our childhood on Carrickard we sat
And viewed the lovely scenery from Curragh to Mullinamac.

Back years five score, souls one hundred and four,
And eighteen dwellings it then did boast
With stalwart men and maidens fair, no equal from coast to coast
But emigration came, we regret the same
and many's a mother sighed
As sons and daughters bade goodbye and sailed out with the tide.

Many houses they stand lonely now, like sentinels they look so sad
Each one could tell a story of good times and of bad
Two smokes are gently rising where a township once did stand

It's folk all gone, forgotten, lost in some foreign land.
No more we have the ceili's in the cottage home so bright
The socials and the card plays to cheer up the winter's
night
The fiddler in the corner as the youngsters danced around
All roads they led to Carrick then from the country all
around.

Away over at Lough-a-Bradan, the forestry can be seen
It has already pushed a spearhead through Carrick fields
so green
And soon it will be timber that will be passing down the
way
In the wake of laughing boys and girls who grew up and
went away.